SHaMaN IN a 9 to 5 WORLD

By Patricia Telesco

THE CROSSING PRESS
FREEDOM, CALIFORNIA

For information on bulk purchases or group discounts for this and other Crossing Press titles, please contact our Special Sales Manager at 800/777-1048.

Visit our website on the Internet: **www.crossingpress.com**

2nd Printing, 2000

Library of Congress Cataloging-in-Publication Data
Telesco, Patricia, 1960-.
    Shaman in a 9 to 5 world / by by Patricia Telesco.
        p. cm.
    Includes bibliographical references.
    ISBN 1-89594-982-2 (pbk.)
    1. Shamanism--Miscellanea. 2. City and town life--Miscellanea. I. Title: Shaman in a nine to five world. II. Title.

BF1621.T44   2000
133.4'3--dc21   99-057496

taBLe of conTents

In 1992 I wrote *Urban Pagan* for people like myself who were struggling to balance city living with metaphysical beliefs and who found themselves wanting. Apparently this book struck a chord that continues to resonate in the magical community. People still tell me how thankful they are to find that they're not alone, and to discover practical ways of expressing magical beliefs, no matter where life takes them.

As they recounted personal stories, these individuals probably had no idea know how deeply their experiences and words affected me. Over six years I have listened, watched, commiserated, discussed, pondered, and learned. I listened to the hundreds of urban pagans whom I met in my travels, each of whom inspired me with creative magical approaches to city living. And I listened when they asked for more books that focus on the city environment and its unique needs.

Shaman in a 9 to 5 World is the answer to that request. It is also a book that my heart yearned to write from the perspective of the person I've become. *Urban Pagan* subscribed to the K.I.S.S. (keep it simple and sublime) school of magic. This book follows suit, but it does so with a maturity and depth of awareness—especially in terms of responsibility—that only more living and magical experience can bring.

As I took up the figurative pen, this book became as much a growth-oriented experience for me as I would want it to be for you. As you read, know that the words of hundreds of others of neopagans and shamans, just like you, echo in these pages. Both I and these kindred spirits are with you in spirit, urging you onward in the journey to successfully finding the shaman within, and expressing that person without.

This book, by its nature, isn't something I could do without the aid of my tribes. So to each of you who has given me hope, a kind word, shared good ideas, and offered motivating nudges when most needed, I send my heartfelt gratitude. My inner shaman is a far better person for having known you all.

foreword

There are many forms of shamanism, ranging from the methods exhibited in Celtic history to the shamanic medicine people of Africa and South America. Each tradition had different rituals, approaches to spellcraft, names for the divine, and variations in philosophy that reflected their unique times and cultures. Despite this variety, some basic commonalities exist with regard to the ideals, roles, responsibilities, and abilities of a shaman within his or her society. I have endeavored to focus on those commonalities in this book.

Shaman in a 9 to 5 World presents a cross-section of shamanic beliefs and practices, or what's currently called core shamanism, as applied in an urban setting. In the process of studying, borrowing, and adapting, I have made every effort to retain the integrity of shamanic practices. This effort acknowledges that some things don't translate well in an urban setting, and that other ideas or techniques are best left untouched out of respect.

After reading this book you may meet people living a shamanic path who do things differently than presented herein. More than likely, that person is practicing one specific form of shamanism with rites and beliefs suited to the tradition from which it originates. Or perhaps she or he has found a personal way of expressing the shaman within. In either case, if that person's approach helps him or her live in harmony with self, the earth, others, and the Sacred powers, then it is an approach deserving of respect.

Those walking a positive spiritual path are all heading in the same direction. It's just that sometimes we take different routes. All those routes are worthy of honor and a safe space within which to experience the Sacred. May your path be free of rocks and potholes, and may this book become a helpful road map along the way.

INTRODUCTION

A shaman stands gazing thoughtfully at the city's horizon. Behind the skyscrapers there lies the path of a well-worn and ancient tradition—a tradition that sees everyday reality and spirituality as part of one sacred circle. Ahead, the future is still unfolding in ways that the Ancestors probably never imagined. Yet in the midst of this rapid transition, the shaman stands firm—cloaked by the leaves of a potted tree, wearing the sky as a hat and the sidewalk for shoes.

This scene won't be found on any greeting card or inside the pages of a novel. Instead, it's one that's playing itself out right now on urban stages across the world. Why? Because the earth's rapidly increasing population and a technologically driven society has left us with fewer and fewer wild regions. Consequently, the shamanic, tribal soul of humankind that yearns to connect with the earth—to know the Mother—is often left to fend for itself in the concrete jungle.

Shaman in a 9 to 5 World was written with this reality in mind. The information and activities in this book provide a step-by-step guide for finding, awakening, and empowering the shaman within. Once that intuitive connection is established, *Shaman in a 9 to 5 World* goes on to present practical, effective ways to master and adapt an urban shamanic lifestyle—a lifestyle that's earth-friendly, socially responsible, and spiritually fulfilling, wherever you may be.

No matter the era or setting in which you find them, the traditional roles and responsibilities of a shaman are that of priest, warrior, teacher, visionary, and healer. *Shaman in a 9 to 5 World* explores each of these roles as they apply to our "strange new world"—a world filled with traffic jams and computers instead of wilderness. From the very first chapter you will become your own priest or priestess by establishing a positive spiritual environment in which to nurture and nourish the shaman within.

Next, in the role of the warrior-priest, you will discover effective ways to safeguard and positively augment the sacred space of self, home, and earth. As a teacher, you'll learn how to share the tradition of urban shamanism with others, especially the children in your life, who represent our future hopes. As the visionary you'll learn various ways of seeing the present and the future through spiritual eyes. Finally, you'll enter the role of a healer, mastering various methods for fostering mental, spiritual, and physical wholeness.

These functions may seem overwhelming at first, but they're not as difficult to integrate as you might think. *Shaman in a 9 to 5 World* encourages simplicity and meaning as the keys to achieving success, not trappings or involved rites. This way we can begin finding time for the Sacred even when faced with busy schedules and numerous responsibilities. Additionally, *Shaman in a 9 to 5 World* advocates updating and modifying our spiritual paths to survive the changes and challenges that face us in the new millennium. This approach effectively blends the best of the past with the present for a potent alliance—an alliance that honors the planet, its people's traditions, inspired innovation, and personal vision.

In a distilled form, *Shaman in a 9 to 5 World* really boils down to thinking and acting differently, and to living in a unique, spiritually centered way every day. Shamanism isn't just about magic. In fact, that's only a small part of a much bigger picture. Shamanic living focuses first on the self—on becoming all that you can be no matter what your life's circumstances or surroundings. Next, shamanism shifts your awareness toward the tribe of people you call family, and your importance in that unit. On a much larger scale, shamanism also stresses the familial tribe of humankind and our need to play nicely together in the sandbox called earth.

Most importantly, shamanic principles redirect our gaze to the Sacred and the Ancestors—the originating powers of creation, and those who have come before us showing the way to a better future by the example of their life. Theirs is the path that *Shaman in a 9 to 5 World* follows: a path carved out by the hand of the gods, tempered by time, energized by magic, and enriched by the vision of each soul who chooses it.

May Spirit walk gently with you on this journey.

the shaman within

Meditation is that exercise of the mind by which it recalls a known truth.

—George Horne

Some shamans are called to the task; some are chosen. Others learn the role through the tradition of their families, and others embark on the shamanic path because it mirrors deep-seated personal beliefs and ideals. No matter how one comes by the title, however, there is no such thing as instant shamanism. Shamanism has aspects that are hidden from all but the serious student, and as a result it takes time, tenacity, and patience to master.

To learn shamanic arts one must embark on a great adventure of seeking, meditating, integrating, changing, and growing. Just as in the storybooks, the best place to start the process is at the beginning. Let's begin with a brief overview of what shamanism is, where it developed, and what practices and beliefs it embodies.

From the perspective of ethnographers, a shaman is one who acquires knowledge or skills by supernatural means, often through rituals or ordeals. Generally, shamanic rituals encourage communion with sacred powers. Ordeals (like walking on hot coals) symbolically allow shamans to "die to the world" so they can receive visions, prophesy, shapeshift, and work other potent forms of magic. People fitting this basic definition appear in numerous culturally diverse societies including the Eskimos of Alaska, the Native Americans, the Celts in Europe, the *Tungus* of Manchuria, the *Yamabushi* of Japan, and even perhaps some people in your own backyard!

The term *shaman* has two potential origins. In Sanskrit the word *sranaba* means an ascetic guided by the powers of spirit(s). This spirit helps the shaman to perform various duties ranging from healing and weather magic to divination and improving a couple's fertility. Another possible origin for shaman is the Tunquso-Manchurian word *saman*, meaning "one who knows." By fusing these two definitions we get a portrait of the shaman as a spiritual messenger to self, individuals, and whole villages about matters affecting everyday life. Shamans were effectively the original priests, physicians, and psychologists all wrapped up in one.

From this same definition, we can also surmise that shamans were wise and clever. They observed nature and people carefully to learn more about the world and how to work effectively in it. In the process, the environment and everything in it was applied as constructively as possible. If something was readily available as a ritual or spell component and had meaning to the shaman or the people he or she served, it was used. If the items and approaches proved successful, they were memorized. This body of knowledge was carefully guarded and passed on through oral tradition to the next person deemed worthy.

As a result, no matter the setting, people trusted the shaman to have a time-honored, reliable, and socially significant answer, be it practical or magical, to the problems at hand. Villages often displayed this trust and admiration by providing for the shaman's daily needs and diligently protecting her or him against harm; it was considered nearly catastrophic to lose the spiritual guardian of any community.

This combination of awareness, observation, sensibility, creativity, and earned trust distills the essence of what the modern urban shaman seeks:

- A deeper awareness of and connection to Spirit, and an intimate awareness of Spirit's guidance

- The ability to express that spiritual relationship through word and deed

- An understanding of, appreciation for, and reunification with the environment on both physical and spiritual terms

- The productive, practical use of that environment in meeting needs or accomplishing positive goals

- The ability to blend personal vision into the spiritual equation to bless everything and everyone the shaman's life touches

In this chapter, I will discuss the basic concepts that I consider useful in developing an urban shamanic lifestyle (more advanced ones, and specific tools and techniques are discussed later in this book). The ideas addressed here appear regularly in shamanic teachings around the world, and they should give you a good idea if the shamanic path is one that you feel comfortable in following. They also create the foundation for all the exercises, activities, and information in the book, making it more readily usable in your life from the start. So please take your time reading this chapter and meditate on each section.

THOUGHTFULNESS AND SILENCE

> *Earth, teach me stillness.*
> —Ute prayer

Here you begin your journey to awakening…a journey that ultimately reveals that light and darkness, sounds and silences, spirit and matter, person and god, are interconnected parts of a greater whole, and also are part of your heart. Like all journeys, however, there's a first step to take, a step toward a different way of thinking, perceiving, and acting. Taking time out for thoughtfulness and silence is that first step.

The concept of practicing purposeful thought and silence is one of the most important philosophies that nearly all shamanic traditions teach. In a world where noise barrages our every waking moment, this practice becomes nothing less than vital. Without making time for quiet thought, we cannot consciously recognize the Sacred and the ways it manifests in our lives. Without silence, we can never hope to hear the still, small voice of the Ancestors or Spirit speaking to our hearts.

Thought

To discover the shaman within yourself, begin with thought. Stop your hurrying for a moment. Slow down and think. Think about your past, about all the moments and people that have touched or changed you. Meditate quietly and deeply on this subject. If it helps, write out your feelings or tape record them. Let all your emotions and memories flow freely.

As you review snapshots from the past, treasure the best parts. Hold tight to the valuable lessons you've learned, and let go of the rest. You do not have to be bound to any negative images or ideas that linger in your conscious mind. You're outgrowing those angers, insecurities, and pains, and moving into a state of renewal. So let them go! Frequently the only barrier between freedom and bondage is untying the rope and refusing to pick it up again. Release yourself and begin building anew, using spiritual vision as the cornerstone to creating a self-actualized urban shaman.

Growth and change is an essential part of life, as is facing our shadows. The light within and that of Spirit will help you banish those shadows and illuminate your potential. The figurative "on switch" for this light lies in a single thought. The thought says "I can." *I can* leave the past behind, taking only what's best on my journey. *I can* learn to promote peace within and without; *I can* be patient with myself and others; *I can* forgive; *I can* learn; *I can* see Spirit in all things. Use these phrases regularly as affirmations of the new person you're becoming. This kind of positive thinking, when supported by word and deed, initiates the first step toward directing personal destiny and reawakening the shamanic self.

Next, think about yourself today, who you are and where you're going. How often do you get caught up in society-trained negativity and stereotypes? Just as you release negative thought forms from the past, don't bind yourself to any current images and ideas that aren't life-affirming. Now is the time to act. *Now* is the power point from which you can make a change, starting from within.

Watch yourself carefully and think about where unhealthy or unproductive reactions come from. Be prepared: You may have to dig deeply to find the root of the problem, but it's well worth the effort. With each successful excavation, you'll begin developing a conscious awareness that breaks old patterns and replaces them with something positive: insightful perspective.

The ultimate manifestation of this awareness comes in your interactions with other people and in specific circumstances. There are always alternatives, always different ways of seeing and approaching things. Using this awareness effectively is one of the urban shaman's goals. Now, instead of knee-jerk, preconditioned actions or reactions, you'll pause for a moment and *think*, "size up" someone or a situation, then act accordingly using wisdom and spiritual discernment as guides. In this manner an urban shaman always remains involved in his or her "village," but he or she is also set apart from it in an important way: apart from going along with the crowd on issues that shape the soul of a person, influence the spirit of whole communities, or affect the earth's sacredness.

Finally, think about the future: your hopes, your dreams, your goals. Are you making positive efforts to fulfill them? Even with the help of Spirit, life is still what we make of it, and nothing is impossible except that in which we cannot believe. An urban shaman looks hopefully toward the horizon ahead, allowing positive energy to flow in that direction, but he or she also knows well the path along which he or she walks. This creates a partnership between aspiration and action, faith and knowledge, Spirit and humankind. It is a potent alliance.

This partnership impacts far more than just the self. If you think of the word thoughtfulness as a compound word (thought-fullness), the effect our thinking has on others becomes clearer. When we think positively, we act differently, and live fully. Consideration and benevolence become part of life's working vocabulary. Call this "random acts of kindness," or call it a rebirth of common courtesy. In either case, the overall effect is that of bringing a little more joy, hope, love, and fullness into the world one person at a time.

Silence

The dictionary defines silence as a state or quality of being in which calm and stillness prevails. Stillness is an in-between place: in between two breaths lies stillness. In between waking and sleeping lies stillness. In between this world and the next lies stillness. When we seek out stillness and silence, we poise ourself in this in-between, very magical place. Here, in a hushed moment of the soul, the normal chatter of the mind is quiet. No words escape our lips, and the daily turmoil stops. Here we come and listen for Spirit's guidance.

With a house that's situated on a city street, and inhabited by many pets and three children, I'm intimately aware of how difficult it can be to find even a brief moment of silence. For myself and my husband, such a moment often comes in the wee hours of the morning. Something will have kept us up, then suddenly we realize the house is totally, blissfully hushed. At that moment, the cares of the day seem to be washed away by peacefulness and a serene joy that permeates the stillness. I've also noticed that this is when spiritual inspiration often strikes—when my world slows down and shuts up long enough for the Divine to get a word in edgewise.

After having experienced silence and its wonders, I highly recommend it as a coping mechanism for city living as well as a spiritual adjunct. It contrasts the days and nights of noise, crowds, responsibilities, and expectations with quiet solitude, restfulness, and no one to impress. Now it is just you and Spirit; rebuild an intimate relationship with both.

At least once a week turn off your radio, television, telephone, and other noisemaking appliances. Put up a "Do not disturb" sign. Ask people not to bother you except for an emergency, then just sit and listen. Listen to the stillness. It speaks far more loudly than one might expect. It resonates with the voice of clarity and wisdom.

Listen to your breath and the beating of your heart. In that rhythm lies part of the universe's cadence. Know it as your own. Listen to the voice within that knows what's best, and learn to trust in it. Most importantly, listen to Spirit and its guidance. Trust me when I say you will know the voice when it comes. This voice ignites the coals of the shaman within—coals that you will continue to carefully tend and strengthen with thought and silence.

TRUTHFULNESS AND REALNESS

A second philosophy widely seen in shamanic beliefs is the importance of honesty. One cannot be a shaman without being constructively true to self and others. From an early age onward, much of my life, and I'm sure yours, has been about hiding behind propriety, behind safe facades, and behind situational personas. Now those masks have to come off. We need to return to the essential self without excuse or remorse.

Truthfulness

The struggle with self-truth often originates with poor self-images or unreasonable expectations. We are, after all, human, with human limitations and failings. But we also bear the remarkable human attribute of curiosity, an amazing capacity for love, and the ability to change not only the self, but the world. So, while you shouldn't blind yourself to shortcomings, don't overlook the good stuff either. The key here is balance. Know your limits and talents. Honestly express both, and work within those boundaries to the best of your ability.

To cite a personal example: Sometimes a publisher calls asking for a book on a specific subject that really isn't suited to my skills and background. As much as I might *want* to say yes, I can't. Truth requires that I don't lie to myself by trying to write about something I don't know or live. Truth requires that I remain responsible for my words and works, even when it's emotionally difficult or financially imprudent to say no.

The struggle that emerges while practicing truth with others often begins in societal contrivance. Many people don't really want to know the truth, which is plainly evident by the superficial nature of most conversations. We smile and ask, how are you? But do most people answer honestly? Probably not. They fear societal reproach and judgment. This is even more potently illustrated in the city, where you're lucky if people communicate at all!

Truthfulness also makes us uneasy because it sacrifices some of our comfortable personal space. You'll notice that an honest person is much easier to get close to both physically and emotionally. That's because peace and harmony can only develop where open, honest, and ethical communication exists. Truth opens the way for that communication so that trust may follow (or at the very least a modicum of respect), but it does so by issuing a challenge. Truthfulness says: Open up and be real!

Realness

Margery Williams expressed the idea of realness beautifully in her book *The Velveteen Rabbit*. When the stuffed animals of this story discuss what it is to be real, they teach us that realness doesn't come by placing people or things on pedestals. It comes from living fully, and from releasing ourselves from unhealthy, outmoded, or unattainable "for-the-sake-ofs."

For the sake of appearances, for the sake of appropriateness: Too many of these "for-the-sake-ofs" bind the shaman within from really expressing, exploring, and experiencing. Sadly, we often don't discover or recognize our realness until later in life, which may be why so shamanic teachings stress honoring the elders. They are real. Their facades have gone the way of age: self-awareness, realness, truthfulness remains.

A good example of realness is reflected in the way we handle interpersonal relationships. It's easy to blame others and sound judgmental when we speak emotionally. Realness, however, asks us to step back and lose the attitudes. Instead of trying to place blame, realness encourages us to state what we feel and why, without condemnation. For example, rather than saying "You never tell me how you feel," you might say "I need to know where I stand." This turns the matter away from pointing fingers to a forthright expression of need.

Even with this example, it's hard to know exactly how to develop truthfulness and realness in a plastic world. Quite possibly the path to accomplishing this takes us around the sacred circle back to step one: thought and silence. Stop to think quietly before you speak or act; think about what words and actions will heal instead of harm; think about what represents the essential, uncensored you; think about how to express this to others without annihilating the truths with which they struggle.

Just like any other spiritual practice, this process becomes more natural with time and persistence, so be patient with yourself. The shaman recognizes that all of life is a journey where you never really "arrive." It's an ongoing progression of plateaus that one can reach, and from which one can certainly fall. Truthfulness and realness is one such plateau.

Old habits are hard to break, and certain situations bait the truthfulness factor like the proverbial carrot before a horse. When you find your words or actions misrepresenting your realness, simply stop, think, and change them. Use this as a learning experience, not one for which to berate yourself.

In the immortal words of the great bard, "To thine own self be true." And stay true. As long as you follow the voice of truth and realness you will not stray far from your path or its goals.

PRESENCE AND ATTENTION

The Master gives himself up to whatever the
moment brings.

—Lao Tzu

The dictionary defines being present as existing now, in this time, in a state of attentive readiness. Bearing this definition in mind, a shaman strives to be ever-present, attentive to, and participatory in his or her life. By giving herself or himself to each moment fully, the shaman lives consciously as the master of her or his destiny.

To put this into a metaphoric illustration, think of each moment of living like one part of a delicious meal. While you consume the allegorical foods that nourish body, mind, and spirit, savor them! Don't idly muse about other buffets and what they might contain. Being present begins here and now, in what's right before you. This moment, this meal, is sacred and important down to the very last bite, and it deserves your complete attention.

This outlook is doubly important for the urban shaman whose

vision of life is constantly bombarded by status quos. Each time you surrender to any unrealistic, meaningless, or demeaning expectation it drains personal power and squelches your inner shaman. Present, attentive living recognizes that it is impossible to achieve a picture-perfect life as measured by an external standard (i.e., family, friends, or society). The only accurate measurement is taken by the internal gauge of a truthful heart.

So, be ever-present and pay attention to what life and Spirit are trying to tell you. Buddha once said that many things in our spiritual life boil down to staying awake. Wake up to who you are and who you wish to become. Wake up to your potential and power. Wake up to see the changing self and appreciate that new being. And finally, stay awake, present, and attentive so that the shaman within can continue to grow and find external expression.

RECOGNITION AND RECONNECTION

The fully awakened, attentive shaman becomes a map maker and keeper for many realms, including the dwelling of the originating force of the universe. It would be impossible to fulfill this role without an intimate belief in, and vision of, the things, places, and connections that exist just beyond normal awareness. There is truly much more to life than meets the eye. For the urban shaman, recognizing this truism is one key component to having a successful, fulfilling spiritual life.

When you drive by a junk yard, look up and see smog, or listen to the racket created by a freeway, it is hard to sense anything remotely sacred. We have to find ways to look beyond this tarnish to see the shining beauty that once was—to see and feel the universal energy in all things. Once we learn how to recognize this power, we can then begin developing a relationship with, or reconnecting with, our tribes, the Ancestors, and the Source of all things: the Great Spirit.

The Great Spirit
We are all children of a great power. Although known by many faces

and names, this power is often designated simply as the Great Spirit, a sacred presence who abides in all things. Whether or not this presence interacts directly with humankind depends on the beliefs of the shamanic tradition studied. Nonetheless, as the creator and binding tie to all things, the Great Spirit will play a role in any shamanic path you undertake. It's up to you to determine what that role will be.

I personally believe that making a place for the Great Spirit in our lives is very important, especially for urban shamans. So much of our existence is literally inundated with concrete, including our thoughts. To awaken our full spiritual potential, our thoughts—motivated by faith—must reach beyond the concrete, beyond the tangible, and touch the heavens once more. It is here, in the places beyond time and dimension, that we will rediscover a sacred spark. Then, like Prometheus, we can bring back this spark, use it to ignite our spiritual power, and push back the darkness in our lives with light.

In my life, I acknowledge the process of recognition and reconnection through a daily ritual. Each morning I light a candle (symbolizing the sacred spark) and greet the Great Spirit with a moment of thanks and quiet thoughtfulness. Sometimes that moment lasts no more than a couple of minutes before having to rush out the door or attend to some chores. Even so, I have still made a place for the Sacred, recognized the importance of that power in my life, and welcomed that presence into my morning. It really changes the tone of my daily life in both subtle and profound ways.

So, try to make room for god/dess. The more space you give to the Great Spirit in your life, the more s/he can touch you, flow through you, and energize the shaman you're becoming every moment.

The Ancestors

The Ancestors are the spirits of people who have passed over. These spirits generally fall into three categories: blood family, indirect family or friends, and historical or histo-mythic figures. Of these, the first category is thought to be the most potent, especially for resolving long-term cycles that harm households and entire tribes.

In many shamanic traditions it's believed that the Ancestors have a greater wisdom from having faced the mystery of death. After passing over, they stay close by to remind us that the past, present, and future are part of the same sacred circle, forever entwined. Customarily, male Ancestors stand near the right side of the body, and female Ancestors stand near the left of the person to whom they're connected. From this positioning, they watch over individuals and entire communities, offering insight into unfamiliar situations and everyday difficulties.

Generally, the Ancestors wait to be recognized and contacted before stepping in with aid. This figurative astral phone call is placed through prayer or during times of stillness, often by simply speaking the Ancestor's complete name. This particular approach ties directly into the important role of names in shamanic communities (see Chapter 4). By knowing a person's name and reciting it reverently, the shaman asks the spirit into the earth-plane where it can then function more fully.

Alternatively, a shaman might sing to the Ancestors, or sound sticks or bones as a call for assistance. No matter the method, though, it is evident that the Ancestors represent an important part of who our inner shaman is, and who we hope to become.

Our society has become very transitory, resulting in the loss of interpersonal connections and family traditions. Recognizing, honoring, and welcoming the Ancestors back into our lives represents one way to begin recovering those losses.

How do we welcome the Ancestors back? Consider recreating your family tree by talking to the elders in your family. Extend the family tree to include close friends who have passed over. If you wish, also add to this lineage any histo-mythic figures who have influenced your thinking deeply. Next, put the tree, or perhaps some photographs and symbolic figurines, in a place of honor (specifically somewhere that you will see it regularly).

At this location leave a candle and small gifts for the spirits of the Ancestors (such as foods or beverages they would have liked in life). Periodically stop here, light the candle, and think about the richness of history that those images represent. Think about the traits these people exhibited that you might wish to develop. Each positive thought honors these individuals' memories, gives their souls peace, and acts like an ongoing invitation for them to stay close, watch, and help as needed.

The Tribe

Shamanic belief systems recognize that all things are connected and that life is a network. This principle is illustrated powerfully by a phrase added to the end of some shamanic prayers: *and all my relations*. This phrase doesn't mean just the shaman's direct blood relatives, but it also includes acquaintances, strangers, plants, animals, and even insects.

We are all part of many tribes—the tribe of family, the tribe of friends, the tribe of community, the tribe of humankind, and the tribe of earth's creatures. Each of these tribes touches and influences the others in subtle and dramatic ways; the connection is inescapable. Thus, recognizing our tribes, reconnecting with them, preserving them with love, and understanding the tribal soul from which we come, is very important to developing and expressing the inner shaman.

Ancient tribal groups were cooperative and somewhat communal in that extended families lived together under one roof. This was the safest and most effective way to ensure the tribe's continuance. Within this structure each person had a place, a role to fulfill, and each person learned the traditions suited to that role. Be it hunting or gathering, weaving or worshipping, the history and ways of the tribe were preserved as was the sense of each individual having importance. Additionally, the tribe provided an ongoing social structure that gave coherence to otherwise tumultuous times.

Looking to modern times I can immediately see where the loss of our close ties—the loss of tribe—has affected us badly. Some people feel submerged in the sea of humanity. They lack direction and motivation, and don't know how to tap the well of personal power. Others feel lonely and disjointed, having no sense of belonging to anything. I see this especially among our youth, and it is a trend that sorely needs reversing.

Recognizing, reclaiming, and reconnecting with tribe is one way of solving this problem. I realize that some people reading this will immediately say things such as, "My family and I don't get along." I'll let you in on a secret: The ancient tribes didn't always get along, and they weren't immune to group dynamics either. The point here is not allowing problems and misunderstandings to sever our ties to the important tribes in our lives. Find a way to forgive, to heal, to bridge the gaps, to communicate. Find a way to preserve your tribe and its traditions.

When this is not possible due to distance or other circumstances, sometimes we have to build tribes from scratch—essentially creating a strong, unified family of choice instead of blood. This building process is showing signs of being reborn at neo-pagan gatherings where groups of people ritually come together and live with each other for days at a time. This atmosphere fosters real community (e.g., the tribe) as long as we keep thoughtfulness and truthfulness as our allies.

Wherever and with whomever we build our tribes, this process gathers and weaves the fibers of self into a supportive structure that nurtures the shaman within. In this structure and among this group of people, we can be real and we can find wholeness. If we think of the word tribe as an anagram for a moment, the power of this unit and how it affects everyone in it becomes much clearer:

Traditions maintained
Relationships and roots
Interaction and interrelatedness
Becomingness and Be-ing
Emotional support and empowerment

Putting these elements together, as you work toward creating or recreating tribe, you preserve your customs and spiritual ideals through oral and written tradition. The relationships and foundations provided by the tribe create an emotionally supportive atmosphere in which growth-oriented interaction occurs. This gives everyone in the tribe the opportunity to find and express his or her true Be-ing, and to start becoming—becoming more spiritually centered, more loving, more tolerant, more whole. So find or restore your tribes. When you do, treasure them and recognize the tremendous blessing that they represent.

The Earth
We are part of this planet's tribe of creatures. Shamans recognize that this planet is a sacred, vital creation that provides sustenance and education. While I will be discussing our relationship with the earth in detail in Chapter 6, it is important to remember throughout this book that one cannot become a shaman *anywhere* without having a right relationship with the Mother. Even when seemingly lost against a backdrop of buildings, the earth is the supportive matrix from which we grow and are nourished. Consequently, when we are not connected to her and when we are not living harmoniously with her, we cannot reach our fullest shamanic potential.

The hard part for urban shamans is a twofold problem: The first comes from a highly disposable society where the apathy bug constantly nips at our heels. It's very easy to get lazy—to toss things out instead of recycling, or to buy items that aren't earth-friendly, for example. Beyond our own personal laziness or neglect, fossil fuel companies fight against making alternative sources (like electric cars) accessible or affordable to those of us who really want to make ecological changes.

Somewhere in between technology and society the shaman gets trapped, feeling like he or she is fighting an uphill battle. This fosters frustration and prompts the temptation to give up. Please don't. Even the smallest gestures can help a lot, and they also keep you in closer touch with the earth's tribe of living beings.

The second problem comes in being able to recognize the earth's voice amidst the daily clamor, and finding ways to really reconnect with the earth despite the glass and metal that separates her from us. Part of this difficulty can be overcome with a change of attitude. Always remember that no matter where you are, the earth is beneath you and above you. It is truly sacred ground that we walk upon, even if it is hidden beneath the sidewalk and the blacktop.

The earth's spirit can be found in the wind, the clouds, and the sunlight. It's there, living, breathing, and speaking with a voice that cannot be silenced by cars or boom boxes. Once you get past the din, you will find that voice waiting patiently for a shaman to hear it; it's waiting for *you*.

PRAYERFULNESS AND THANKFULNESS

> *Teach me again the simple ways, Great Spirit*
> *teach me to pray.*
>
> —The LoreSinger

Shamans use prayer as a technique for connecting with the Sacred and drawing its energies into everyday life. To honor the earth, they pray for the souls of the animals that give their lives so that we may eat. To support their village, they pray for the tribe and its continuance. To encourage personal growth, they pray for the self, to know a gentle voice. This prayerfulness is far more than just an act of supplication, however. It manifests in the way a shaman thinks and lives.

Prayerfulness constitutes a reverent, respectful attitude and behavior that translates into any situation.

Prayerful thought differs from meditation in that while meditation is an inner conversation, prayer initiates a conversation directly with Spirit. Some prayers ask for aid, other prayers express appreciation for one's blessings or exalt the Divine, and some invoke a purposeful presence. No matter the goal, however, prayer is the song of one's soul to its creator. In prayerful moments we connect with the nucleus of our faith, and all the potentials and possibilities that lie just beyond everyday awareness.

Prayers for aid express our needs and hopes. There is nothing wrong with telling Spirit what you want. Just realize that what you *want* isn't always good for you. This is where the shaman learns acceptance and receptivity. Should Spirit answer a prayer differently than expected, he or she accepts that wisdom, receives it, and integrates the lesson therein.

Thankful prayers are those that show gratitude for our blessings, great and small. Among families, this is a time to appreciate the binding tie of faith, their blessings, and the love and unity that both generate. For individuals, this prayer acknowledges the gift that every day of living represents, as well as an appreciation for the things that make life a little nicer.

Invocations act as a kind of spiritual invitation. These request the interaction, intervention, or intercommunication from powers like the Ancestors and the elements. This isn't done haphazardly, without serious thought, or without a thorough knowledge of *who* you're dealing with. Whatever archetype you call upon in invoking prayers must be suited to the particular time and task, and the task should be something *important*. Just as you wouldn't dial 911 for help with a hangnail, invoking the greater powers should be reserved for times of pressing need.

Once we understand the importance and types of prayer, the

question then becomes: How do I pray effectively? You would think that prayer would come naturally, but it doesn't seem to. A lot of people feel awkward about praying. The idea reminds them of church and rote liturgies that suffocated the inner shaman's creative, expressive voice. For individuals who find themselves in this situation, relax. The prayers of a shaman come from the heart, not from a book or the pulpit.

Other people may feel shy about praying, as if they aren't worthy of Spirit's attention. In looking at my own childhood, this seemed to be the case. I always prayed for others, but not for myself. One of the goals of *Shaman in a 9 to 5 World* is to help you see each person (that means *you*, too) as a sacred, important creation. When we pray for ourselves, we acknowledge our importance, and we ignite the spark of Spirit within so that it can shine throughout the day.

Begin your prayers as this chapter began, then, with thoughtfulness and silence. You cannot pray with intention unless other mental clutter is stilled. Also begin with truth. Spirit knows you as intimately as a parent knows a child. So dispense with any pretenses. Forego King James-style verses, and just use words that are comfortable on your lips—and say what you feel.

Next, be earnest, reverent, humble, and patient. Earnestness gets the universe's attention. Reverence is something that Spirit should always receive from us. To revere something means to honor it and not take it for granted. Humility keeps us aware of the fact that our voice is but one of millions, all of whom have needs. Spirit hears us all, but answers need before desire. Patience makes the waiting easier. Prayer rarely exhibits instantaneous manifestation. Instead, it creates a wave of energy that must reach the right source and then return with an answer. Patience becomes an important helpmate to identifying a response to prayer—whenever, wherever, and however it comes.

The final aspect of prayer comes in the form of thankfulness.

A thankful heart is one ready to fully give and receive. When we don't appreciate our magic, something in it dies; similarly, when we don't appreciate Spirit, it stops speaking. When answers come from prayerful moments, remember to say thank you. Find the voice of gratitude within and let it ring out sure and strong. Be it for the sunrise, health, a good job, or just a quiet moment to listen—give thanks.

INITIATION AND INTEGRATION

For all its insights and wisdom, philosophy does little good if we don't activate it in our lives and integrate its associated lessons. An initiation helps with the activation process. In nearly all religious traditions some form of initiation ritual marks the beginning of a spiritual path. During the rite, a person is formally introduced to the Sacred and symbolically declares her or his intentions to follow that path.

Shamanic traditions are no exception to the initiation process. Upon reaching a certain age, youths undergo a rite of passage that initiates them into adulthood. Upon accepting the shamanic path, adults also undergo some form of initiation. The form this ritual takes varies dramatically from tribe to tribe, but in all cases the goal is the same: accessing and activating the individual's full magical and spiritual potential.

The pathworking rituals that follow are designed to act as a self-guided introduction into the urban shamanic tradition—a simplified initiation, if you will. In modern metaphysical traditions, pathworking is a type of intense meditation and visualization in which the pathworker plays an integral role in the way the exercise unfolds. When you feel ready, willing, and able, use the following activity as a way of accepting the shaman within and welcoming Spirit's guidance in your life's journey.

This exercise opens psychic doorways and starts showing you how to safely navigate the realm of Spirit. Since this process is somewhat detailed, you might want to try tape recording the exercise with pauses at the indicated places. Alternatively, if your own voice distracts you, ask a friend or companion to tape it. This will free up your mind from the task of remembering the details and allow it to focus directly on the experience.

Note: Please don't enter into this activity without some serious thought. Shamanism isn't a path suited to everyone. However, if you've found that the ideas in this chapter mirror what's in your heart, then move forward and use this activity as a way of watering the spiritual seed that already exists in your soul.

A Shamanic Pathworking

PREPARATION: If physically feasible, fast for at least one day before embarking on this journey. Drink plenty of water to cleanse your body, and also take a ritual bath with purifying herbs such as lemon and sage.

Find a comfortable way of sitting that doesn't make you sleepy. Take precautions to ensure that you won't be disturbed. If possible, travel to a quiet natural location so that you can gather the roots of your shamanic self, and then bring them back with you to plant in the city.

TIMING: Dawn is a good choice, being a time that hinges between night and day and one that signals a new beginning.

THE PATH: Close your eyes and relax fully. Breath deeply and slowly, allowing the cares of the day to fall away until nothing exists but your breath and the beating of your heart. When you feel yourself reaching that point of mental stillness, visualize a doorway before you. In front of the door a guardian stands, stern and firm. The guardian asks you why you have come. [Pause and give yourself time to answer. The guardian will not allow you to pass through the doorway until your answer is complete in your own mind and heart.]

The guardian steps back. You now notice that the door seems to have no handle or knob. On closer inspection, however, there is a hand-shaped imprint on the door. You reach out to touch that spot, knowing that once you do, there is no going back. This door opens into the spirit world, and it is your choice to go forward or not [pause to make that choice].

As you touch the imprint, a shiver goes through you. Your hand nearly goes straight through the door as it dissolves. Before you lies a well-worn path. You can tell that many, many people have walked this way before, and many will come after you. All around the path the vista is gray, swirling fog that twists and sparkles with life.

As you move slowly forward and try to adjust your vision, you notice the fog slowly dispersing. The further along the path you walk, the clearer the landscape becomes. You are deep within an ancient forest. All around, trees stand in a circle as if gathered there just for you. Turn completely around once and greet them. These nature spirits will remain here to watch over and protect you until your journey is complete [pause].

As you complete your greeting you notice another huge tree in the center of this circle. It is so large that you cannot see where the branches end and the sky begins. Go to that tree, sit beneath it [pause], and wait in silence [pause].

Eventually, almost imperceptibly, you notice small vines and roots attaching themselves to your body. They are embracing you lovingly and carrying your spirit to beneath the soil. You are now entering the lower worlds. This is the womb of the earth, and a place of beginnings. The soil surrounds you with energy and life. It saturates your skin, becoming part of you, and you become part of it.

You are one with the world tree above, and can feel its life. You are one with the Mother. Here you will discover the part of reality that often eludes you, lying just beneath the surface of what you can physically see. Look around now and see whatever the earth spirit wishes to show you [pause].

This is also the region of the animistic self, the wild person who is filled with instinct and raw drive. Feel the power and presence of the animal-human, and notice how your senses seem heightened. You can smell things, feel things on the edge of your awareness that weren't there before. What do you smell? What do you sense? [pause]

Suddenly you realize that the vines and roots are speaking to you. They whisper your name again and again, asking if you want to go on…if you wish to travel to the middle world. Answer them [pause].

When you say yes, the roots respond by gently pushing you back up to the grove where you began. You emerge from the soil like a butterfly breaking free of its cocoon. The trees around have all bent low to watch over you, all but the great tree whose roots bear you. The backdrop of green is nearly seamless, like a movie screen. This is the middle world upon which your life and experiences can play themselves out in such a way that you can watch and learn. Wait for a moment and see what you most need to understand…see what the tapestry paints for you…become one with life [pause].

After the images stop forming, you notice that it is not the leaves creating the pictures, but small colorful beings who dance and spin. Some appear like raindrops, others like flames, still others like seeds and soil, and others you can only detect by the song in their wings. These are the nature spirits of the middle world. Introduce yourself to them and listen to any messages they have for you. They are excellent guides and helpmates in your shamanic travels [pause].

When the nature spirits are done, they will disappear back into the leaves. Darkness surrounds you like a cloak. There are now no images, no colors. Only your breath and the beating of your heart seem to keep you company. Yet out of this quiet, out of this darkness, you hear something. Music…a song…high above you. It is indescribably beautiful and yet haunting. It speaks of things you've only dared to dream about. It whispers of the universe's mysteries. Do you want to follow that music? [pause to decide]

Looking at the great tree, the closest branch seems nearly impossible to reach. You jump and miss. You jump again and miss.

Finally, on the third try you jump with all your heart and spirit and nearly fly through the air, grasping the branch tightly. Pull yourself up and stay on that branch until you feel balanced and sure of your footing [pause]. Now reach up again. Take the next branch. Take your time and move from one branch to the next and the next until your climb takes you into the clouds.

Stop here for a moment. You are about to enter the upper world, where the heavens, the stars, and all of creation dance together. You do not need your physical body to ascend this part of the tree. Let that image fall off of you, leaving behind a radiant being of light. Release yourself from worldly things and thinking. You are about to embrace the stars; you are about to touch the eternal [pause].

As your body falls away, you feel an amazing sense of freedom. You know that you could go anywhere with but a thought or a wish, but now is not the time. If you have any special spirit guides or teachers, they may choose to make themselves known to you now. Pause and welcome them. Pause and greet the Ancestors. Pause and honor the Great Spirit. Pause and acknowledge yourself as part of life's great tapestry. All things, all people, all places are here and now [pause].

When you stop to look, you can see that the great tree remains below your feet, while all around you a galaxy of power swirls with a rainbow of sparkling light. One of those sparks lands in the area of your third eye and bathes you in energy [pause]. You can feel your power centers opening; you can feel the godself within waking up [pause].

As the power flows through you, your attention is drawn back to the song around you. Listen closely to the music here. It is your shaman's song. Memorize each note. Hum it over and over. Feel its vibrations in every part of your light being. This is the music that you will use again to travel into Spirit. This is the music that you can use for healing, for teaching, for visions. This is the music of the spheres as it mingles with your soul. It is your personal song of power and praise [pause].

At some point you will know it is time to leave. The energy around you will begin to wane and the galaxy will slowly solidify, merging into the upper branches of the great tree. As you move down the branches, allow your breathing to start returning to its normal pace. Leave the forest following the same path by which you came. As the door closes behind you, know that it is always there. You can come back to this place anytime to renew your inner shaman and travel the spirit world.

Open your eyes. Look to the horizon, which now should be filled with light. Greet the day with expectation and make notes of your experiences. At this time, you may wish to set down some type of written promise and accept a personal taboo, which is very traditional. The vow embodies a contract between you and Spirit. Exactly what this promise says is up to your heart to determine, but keep it in a safe place and read it regularly. Allow the written words to inspire you, and to keep your path straight and sure.

As for the taboo, many shamans give up something in order to receive their power and gifts. While the Great Spirit doesn't require such sacrifice, offerings of this nature are very powerful and represent a strong personal commitment. They can also directly represent shamanic beliefs. For example, many urban shamans give up eating meat to honor the Mother and the earth's tribe of living creatures.

Whatever your promise, and whatever your taboo, today marks a fresh start in your life. Move forward now, keeping an image of the shaman you're already becoming safe in your heart. From this point onward, your life will change in wonderful and interesting ways. So be prepared, stay awake, sing your song, and celebrate!

JOYFUL, CREATIVE LIVING

During your efforts to uncover and empower the shaman within, you're likely to fail, get frustrated, and possibly want to give up altogether. When those moments come, use good humor, happiness, and a healthy portion of ingenuity as coping mechanisms. Our Ancestors recognized that laughter really is good medicine. There's little in life that a heart full of joy can't tackle creatively. So, don't let your spiritual growth be paralyzed by life's ups and downs.

Confucius once said that it does not matter how slowly you go so long as you do not stop. Life is a pilgrimage that each person has to take at her or his own pace. This isn't about keeping up with the Joneses—it's about quality learning. The path to true knowledge never ceases until we do. So trust yourself and forge ahead with confidence and joy.

CHAPTER 2

Ritual

What is powerful becomes natural.

—Lao Tzu

In shamanic practices, ritual is not just about illustrating a specific belief or cycle, it's about fulfillment. Rituals consummate the connection between the temporal and spiritual worlds, and therefore help us fulfill our role as ministers and guides to other realms. Rituals also maintain the delicate harmony between humans, the earth, and the Sacred by keeping us attuned and aware of life's rhythm. As such, rituals are an essential part of any shamanic path you undertake.

The root word for ritual means "to fit together." Through drama and song, cadence, dance, and various other components, shamans ritually fit together pieces of energy that become the essence and pattern of life. Without these pieces, the earth cannot move, the tribe cannot continue, and the magic ceases. This chapter reviews the tools and methods of shamanic ritual, so that you can learn how to fit them together effectively in a variety of environments.

Before you get nervous about becoming your own priest or priestess, or the ritual leader for a group, realize that much of your life already has a ritualistic nature. You regularly follow the same routes to work, use the same coffee cup, prepare foods in specific ways, celebrate birthdays ritually, commemorate holidays ritually, honor passages ritually, and so forth. The only real difference is that now you will be *consciously* creating a behavior—"fitting together" a mode of sacred expression—suited to urban shamanism.

EFFECTIVE RITUAL CONSTRUCTS

> *What has arrived is in its place, and what*
> *waits shall be in its place.*
>
> —Walt Whitman

A large majority of shamanic practices and lessons take place in a ritual construct. Within this construct, the shaman is the leader and guide. He or she is one who knows how to create the sacred energies necessary for any occasion or need. In the process, the shaman becomes the center of a cosmic dance that awakens all the power and potential of Spirit within himself or herself, and inspires participants to follow suit. Before looking at the specific tools and techniques that make up a ritual's "blood," it helps to know what basic constructs a ritual's "body" should have.

FIVE KEY CONSTRUCTS FOR EFFECTIVE RITUAL

1 A defined beginning that sets the tone for the ritual and designates sacred space.

2 Strong sensory input, each part of which represents the ritual's goal symbolically or literally.

3 A defined pattern that gets followed closely each time that ritual is performed.

4 Meaningful location, decorations, and other "blood" elements that create a sympathetic environment within which the ritual's theme unfolds.

5 A defined ending that provides closure and grounds the participants.

First, rituals need to have a defined beginning. Whatever marks the start of the ritual also designates the line between world and not world, and prepares the participants for what's about to occur. Good examples here include the lighting of a ritual fire or holding hands in a circle while breathing in unison.

This is also the time when the shaman calls upon guardian energies and the Sacred for assistance, protection, and participation, similar to an invocation in Wiccan tradition (to invoke means to invite). These guardians include those who protect the threshold between worlds, natural spirits, directional or elemental spirits, and/or spirits who walk with the shaman as companions and guides. In many instances, the shaman's animal totem is called upon at this time as well.

Exactly what words, actions, and directional correspondences an invocation uses depends heavily on the type of ritual involved and/or its originating culture. For example, the words and actions for a coming-of-age invocation will differ from those for a house cleansing. Similarly, while many shamanic systems associate North with the air element, Wiccans associate East with air. What's most important here isn't the logistics, but finding a meaningful way to honor the four corners of creation, the Creator, and to welcome those energies into your observance. This effort creates a sacred space, one that has been set aside and consecrated.

Second, rituals need strong sensory input. Sounds, aromas, textures, and sights all affect the way we feel and react in the sacred space. Sensual cues gently guide our minds away from the temporal

terms of other logistics, such as space constraints. Circle dances are pretty difficult to navigate safely in a small apartment, so songs or clapping might substitute. Similarly, someone with allergies might avoid smudge sticks for purifying the sacred space and might use saltwater instead. Please bear these kinds of factors in mind as you read this section, so you can make the best choices for any ritual you lead or create.

Altar

An altar represents the intersection between worlds. In ancient times altars were often made from a convenient stone or other handy flat surface upon which tools were laid and offerings placed. This didn't mean the area was any less sacred—just less fancy—which suits the urban shaman's philosophy perfectly.

Since most things on a shaman's altar come from nature, the altar becomes a marvelously subtle way of expressing spirituality without alarming people who wouldn't understand your choice of belief systems. Then, too, an effective ritual altar doesn't have to be a permanent fixture in your home. I have a friend, for example, who uses a small decorative, lockable box in which she houses tools and components. The additional benefit in this design is portability. My friend transports her ritual tools in the box, using the top for the altar, for the times when she might otherwise miss a celebration due to location (like a hotel) or other circumstances.

Following suit, there's nothing that says you can't use the floor or other readily available surfaces as an altar. Among Peruvian shamans, for example, it is common to hand down a piece of sacred cloth within which tools are wrapped and carried as needed. This cloth, often tattered with age, becomes the altar, no matter where the shaman has to travel.

Remember: Designating sacred space isn't about what you use, it's about attitude. Any place can become an altar if you treat it respectfully. Similarly, anything can become a potent ritual tool if it reflects your inherent power and potential. What items immediately remind you of something you've overcome? Which ones reflect moments when your life became far more than you ever expected it could? These items are good choices for altar decorations and/or tools if for no other reason than reminding you that nothing's impossible!

Aromatics

Aromatics have played an important role in nearly every religious tradition as purifiers, offerings, and symbolic representations of the prayers of the faithful. Shamans specifically use sage, cedar, sweet-grass, lavender, pine, and tobacco, along with a handful of regional flowers. Sage and cedar feature heavily in ritual purification to clear the air of any residual energies and in healing rites. Cedar also balances energy. Sweetgrass smoke pleases the spirits. Pine smoke brings blessings. Tobacco restores our connection with the spirit realm, and was often used as a strewing herb in shamanic holy sites or as an offering to the four winds.

In using these or other aromatics, do whatever you can to ensure that they are organically grown. In metaphysical beliefs, as an herb burns it releases its energy into the area in which you're working. From a shamanic viewpoint, fire liberates the plant's spirit, giving it full expression in the sacred space. In either case, you don't want chemicals misdirecting or inhibiting the vibrations the herbs create, or the magic of your ritual.

Circle

Shamanic rituals take place in a circle. This configuration stresses equality and the intimate connection between the Creator and creation. Within this space, all participants in the circle are free to express and share knowledge. Here, each person has value and is acknowledged as an important part of the tribe.

A circle may be formed in any number of ways suited to your

ritual's setting. Indoors or out, you can place items or markings around an area to demarcate the circle's perimeter. The participants themselves can create a circle simply by holding hands. Outdoors, any natural circle like a grove of trees is an excellent choice for a ritual gathering. Indoors, visualization and directed energy can also mark the edge of the circle's perimeter.

This last approach is probably the easiest, especially if you're working alone or in an area with restricted space. Stand at the center point of the circle you're creating. Close your eyes and breath deeply. Visualize a fountain of luminous, rainbow-colored energy pouring down into your crown chakra. As it saturates your being, stretch out your hands toward the East. Let the energy stream through you to that point, then slowly start turning yourself clockwise, continuing to keep your hands extended.

When you've completed this circle, raise your hands above your head and slowly open them. Imagine the light-energy pouring out of your hands to create a dome above your head. Keep opening your hands in a full circle so they meet again in front of you. As they meet, visualize a sheet of power forming below your feet. In the end you will have a bubble (a three-dimensional circle) of protective light energy within which to work.

At the end of the ritual, reverse the process by drawing in the wards (the protective powers and marks), and returning the energy to the Source. If you used tokens or markings for the circle, reverently put these away or clean the region. If working outdoors, leave the natural circle as clean and untouched as when you arrived.

Costume

Japanese shamans wore feathered cloaks to facilitate the spirit's flight across the veil for soul journeys. North American Indians donned eagle feathers during war rituals to evoke this creature's endurance and speed. In both cases, and in other similar uses of guises, the costumes are not merely decorative, but a potent tool for achieving a ritual's goal.

Costumes represent a mythic process where there is no distinction between reality and other spheres. The costumed person *becomes* what he or she represents. In this manner, costumes create a meeting ground between the natural and magical realms. This helps the shaman break through any barriers that keep these two realms from touching during everyday life.

In modern metaphysical traditions costuming has gone a little by the wayside, probably because many of us have forgotten how to play, imagine, and imitate. Hopefully I can help encourage a revival. Start by thinking about your ritual's theme and any symbols that immediately come to mind. Costumes need to somehow represent your understanding of a ritual and its significance, and these symbols will often provide you with a foundation from which to work.

Next, find readily available pieces of clothing, jewelry, and craft items that reflect the symbolism desired. Put these together creatively, allowing your vision of the ritual to guide you. For the urban shaman costuming doesn't have to be elaborate to work effectively. In fact, sometimes the subtle approach proves more potent on a subconscious level. For example, during Summer Solstice, don gold, yellow, and red clothing or jewelry that represents the sun in its glory. Let the vibrations of the colors heighten your awareness of the sun and the element of fire.

To go a little further, when circumstances and time allows, cut long strips of yellow cloth or ribbon and pin them to your sleeves so they look like streaming sunlight. Use non-toxic body paints to color the visible parts of your body in the same tones. Once assembled, a well-considered costume like this will help you push past the self and connect with the energies it represents. In many ways, this is the old axiom of "clothes make the person" on a metaphysical level.

Before you know it, you'll look and feel like the radiant sun this ritual commemorates!

In similar fashion, any ritual can be transformed into an extraordinary experience through the use of costumes, from subtle ones to the sublime. Give it a try! Additionally, for children, ritual costumes represent a fun way for them to get involved in your tribe's traditions (see Chapter 7, "The Papoose: Children of the Tribe").

Dance

If I can walk, I can dance.

—Old African saying

In cultures as different and widespread as those of Persia and Mexico, dance has been used as a way of honoring the spirits and joyfully releasing the shaman from temporal consciousness. By matching physical motion with sound and intention, ritual dances create harmonious energy and transport the dancer into altered states. Here we begin in the body to go beyond the body; we release ourselves to really feel, to experience, to move in pattern and rhythm with the cosmos.

In shamanism, each dance's motion and rhythm has meaning, and each is meant to unite matter with Spirit. Some dances reflect goals, others inspire the intuitive process, and still others bring us back in touch with our primal instincts. Some dances are done solo, while others take an entire group of people through a process that builds and releases energy.

GUIDELINES FOR RITUAL DANCING

1 Start with a warm-up. Gently stretch your muscles, shake out your arms and legs, and spin a bit to get used to moving in a circle without losing your balance.

2 Try different movements and see how they make you feel. Generally, fluid movement expresses emotions and helps you "go with the flow."

Abrupt movement is full of power and goal-oriented. Fast, ecstatic movement generates energy for manifesting goals, and theatrical movement symbolically expresses your desires as accomplished feats (see the section on Imitation). Make notes of your experience with each type of movement after you try it. Compare these impressions with other people if you're going to be dancing in a group.

3 Using what you discovered in practice, focus on your intention, and choose a pattern. Know, however, that ritual dance is a creative expression of what's happening inwardly, so it may not follow the exact pattern you've chosen. The only reason for pre-determining any format is to give yourself a meaningful place to begin. In a group, the format keeps people from tripping over one another.

4 Use your voice (songs and chanting), music, or other rhythmic expressions as helpmates when you feel awkward or unable to focus. Sometimes all we need is a little nudge to motivate ecstatic release. If you're thinking about the music (or other sensual cues) instead of being in the physical, you're far more likely to experience successful ritual dancing.

5 Let go and listen to the rhythm in yourself, that created by any accompaniment, and Spirit's lyrical voice. Allow your body to feel that vibration down to the very core of your being. Let yourself then physically express what you're feeling. Try not to think about it consciously. Just allow the energy to flow naturally from heart and soul to every part of your body.

   In a group, circle or line dances are most common, and the patterns are often designated by tradition. What's nice, however, is that even when someone doesn't know the "right movements," any attempt at following the pattern supports the growing energy. So try not to get overly self-conscious if you miss a step or two of a weaving dance for Beltane, or just manage to keep up with a speedy clockwise dance of power. Your intention and unity with the group is more important than your precision.

6 At some point you will know the ritual dance is done. Usually it will reach a climax, then slowly wind down like a music box's spring.

When it's over, relax and integrate the experience. Be forewarned that unexpected emotions can surface at this time. Our bodies remember things even when we do not, and ritual dancing can release those memories. Write in your spiritual journal about what you feel, about the dance, about imagery that came to you, and anything else you think is important. Refer to this in the future when choosing patterns for ritual dancing.

Drumming

Drums are perhaps the most important shamanic tool, found in diverse traditions ranging from those of Siberia and Africa to that of the Native Americans. In every location, the sound of the shaman's drum transports him or her to other realms, and helps other people to follow. The sound of the drum focuses the shaman's resolve and attention, and bridges the gap between temporal and spiritual modes of thought.

I will be discussing finding or making drums in Chapter 9, but briefly it is important to know that nearly every shaman I spoke to said that his or her drum "found" him or her, not vice versa. Something about the tone, shape, or spirit of the drum called to that person loudly. So while I'd hazard to say a shaman's kit isn't complete without a drum, don't go running out and buy the first one you see. Wait, listen, and watch for the *right* drum to come to you.

Once you find a drum, you may wish to decorate it in some manner that designates it as your own. Feathers, bells, crystals, and other small tokens that hang from the sides of the drum can augment its power and reflect your intimate connection with this tool. Beyond this, regularly stroking the drum head with your hands puts natural oil into the surface and marks the drum with your personal energy.

In speaking with Don Waterhawk, a friend of mine whose drumming I respect tremendously, I discovered that the head of the drum represents a sacred circle in many shamanic traditions. Each quarter of the circle corresponds with a direction or element. So, I honored those elements by decorating my drum with bells (air), a foxtail (earth), shells (water), and incense (fire).

Don says that each region of the circle also has a distinctive voice. He recommends that you start any drumming session from the East—so your music is always filled with hope. He rarely uses the western quarter of his drum, however, as that's the traditional place of the Ancestors. One does not speak with the Ancestor's voice unless guided to do so.

Beyond these basic guidelines, the essential key to drumming is listening. If drumming alone, listen to your heartbeat and the rhythm of life all around you. Respond to that cadence, and blend it with the voice of the drum. Drumming is never really a solo experience. It brings together Spirit and person inside the echo of each vibration. Every drumbeat is like a word—it expresses something specific, and it carries power. So keep your goals in mind while you work.

In a group setting, listen to the other drummers. This is not a competition where one should overwhelm the other. Let yourself move into a meditative state where you are united with your tribe, united with your drum's spirit, and then play accordingly. Many people find they experience far deeper trance states in the confines of a good drumming circle. That is because the drum creates a resonance with the cycles of time, the circle of your tribe, and the power of Spirit.

Fire

In many instances a ritual altar was abandoned in favor of using the earth as a table, and having a central ritual fire mark the place where worlds meet. I rather favor this approach, but it doesn't always work well in an urban setting. One compromise might be to have the altar table in the center of your working space with a candle or brazier on it. The candle/brazier takes the place of the ritual fire.

The ritual fire represents more than a figurative altar, however. Fire provides light, it consumes darkness, it warms, it lives fully. In these four qualities fire gives us important lessons individually and as a tribe. Around the light of a fire, the tribe gathers in equality. Through the light of the fire, our souls are illuminated. As the fire consumes the wood and the darkness, it can also consume our negativity and our doubts. As it warms, our spirits and hearts find it possible to reach out with warmth and love. As it lives fully, so should we.

Here's one way to bless yourself with a ritual fire. At some point during a ritual, give the fire an offering that symbolizes something from which you want to be freed. Let the fire consume that item and liberate your soul. Afterward, quickly (and carefully) pass your strong hand through the fire and back (perhaps dampen it first for safety). Touch this hand to your heart so Spirit's fire and consciousness abides there. Also pass your hand through and back two more times, touching your crown chakra and third eye respectively, so that the paths to Spirit's knowledge and discernment remain open and energized. Thank the Fire Spirit for its help and continue with your ritual.

Note that this basic procedure can be changed depending on the goal of your ritual. You might, for example, wish to touch your feet with fire energy to motivate change and shine a light on the parts of your path that seem elusive. Or, touch your pelvic region when you're having trouble physically expressing love and passion (see Chapter 5).

Fasting and Food

Some rituals suggest fasting (when physically feasible) for a certain period beforehand so that your body and auric field get a good housecleaning. Symbolically, fasting represents putting away the mundane world and physical needs in favor of the spiritual self. In simpler terms, fasting creates a purer vessel through which sacred energy can flow without hindrance.

Balancing this, feasts often follow a ritual as a way of rejoicing and fellowshipping with tribe. In the process, the body receives necessary nourishment, just as one's spirit did by fasting. Additionally, food helps ground out participants who may not have fully anchored themselves back into the physical realm. Finally, symbolically chosen food helps people internalize the theme of a ritual so that its energy will linger long afterward.

Imitation

Shamans use symbolic, imitative movements in ritual to honor a power, unite with that power, and release the associated energy. For example, it is common in planting rituals to include a jumping dance meant to inspire the crops to grow high. Similarly, before a hunting expedition an elaborate ritual pantomime might be enacted, ending with a victorious capture. Both these examples illustrate a strong shamanic belief that manifestation follows intention and action.

To understand imitative magic more fully, think back to your youth for a moment. As children we imitate to learn. Through imitation comes experience, awareness, and eventual attainment. Imitative magic is basically the same. You reverently imitate a power to understand and learn about it. Afterward you're more attuned and can direct the associated energy more effectively toward the ritual's goals.

The urban shaman faces some difficulties in magical mimicry, often being surrounded by prying eyes. Nonetheless, I think that there are ways to adapt the concept effectively. For example, before doing a ritual for prosperity, live a little more abundantly. Buy something "luxurious" for yourself, or splurge on gourmet food. Living this way sets up sympathetic energy that is further empowered by the ritual.

Other examples? Well, rather than doing a jumping dance when you plant a garden, how about wearing predominantly green clothing or a shirt filled with flowers? Both of these visually imitate the energy that you want for your garden—green, growing, and fruitful! Or, when trying to "hunt down" something specific, put an image of what you're looking for across the room, and slowly move toward it throughout the ritual. By the end of the ritual, take the object in hand to "grasp" success!

Masks

> *[The mask] is used at those times when human*
> *experience is transforming.*
> —John Mack, *Masks and the Art of Expression*

The use of masks as a shamanic tool is very ancient. Historical evidence suggests that shamans may have used masks as early as the Paleolithic era for sympathetic hunting, harvest, and healing magic. The reason for using a mask varied (as did the corresponding visage) depending on a ritual's goal, but its popularity among tribal, shamanic cultures remained constant.

Traditionally, masks delivered a visible face for folk heroes, potent spirits, and the gods. For example, some shamans used a mask when effecting cures. The hope in doing so was to better relate to the represented Spirit's force, become possessed, and thereby produce miracles. The mask served an alternative function here of providing inspiration to the patient. Instead of seeing good old "Joe" before them, who might not inspire any type of emotional response, the mask transformed the shaman into a formidable sight.

Today, masks remain a way to explore the depths of human imagination. Here, for a few moments the shaman can retreat from "normalcy" and explore limitless possibilities. From this vantage point he or she gains unique perspectives into animals, plants, situations, and people. In fact, urban shamanic mask making and wearing has taken interesting and creative turns in recent years.

Women sometimes make pregnancy masks to channel positive energy to an unborn child. The finished mask then doubles as a ritual bowl for use in any ceremonies for the child in the future. Someone wanting to overcome bad habits or fears might make an ugly mask that gets taken off and destroyed in ritual. These are but two good examples of the many ways you can ritually use masks.

While you might feel awkward at first about making and wearing a mask, remember that we all wear figurative masks from time to time. We put on a "happy face" or wear contact lenses to make ourselves feel more attractive. So adapt this technique to your goal of connecting with shamanic energies in any way you feel is appropriate. Honor your animal guide (see Chapter 4), protect your home (see Chapter 3), or banish a negative habit by destroying an ugly mask. No matter what their final form or function is, let your ritual masks express the force that walks with you every day with or without a guise.

Offerings and Sacrifice

The tradition of leaving offerings for the gods and goddesses, or making sacrifices to them, is tremendously ancient. While it is difficult for us to fully understand the blood sacrifices of our Ancestors, we can understand the principle behind them. One must be willing to give in order to receive.

Offerings can take any form, but should be as earth-friendly as possible. If you're giving some bread from your table, for example, scatter it for the birds. If making an offering of a favorite piece of clothing, pass it along to someone in need. *Intention* is the key. Even though the bread goes to the birds, and the clothing goes to a person, the gift's intention is one of honoring and propitiating Spirit.

Some offerings, such as herbs, can be burnt. The smoke generated blesses the ritual space with its energies. Other offerings can come through deeds. For example, give up a favorite food for a week before a personally important ritual. This "giving away" should be as significant as you can make it. The more you treasure your offering, and the more relevance it has with regard to the ritual, the more potent the results will be.

To cite a personal example, during financially trying times I'll offer something I treasure to the universe by promising to sell it during the prosperity ritual. Once when we needed to pay the rent, for example, I sold an antique dagger that was part of my ritual kit. While making that offering was difficult at first, the results from the effort were incredibly fulfilling to me. A better job came through shortly after the sale.

Since shamans don't tithe, per se, you can consider this a kind of spiritual tithe. Offerings represent a meaningful way to give back something to Spirit and say "thanks." Some things in magic, as in life, also carry a price. That price might be anything from giving up some personal time to giving away worldly goods. Whatever the cost, however, it is always fair, and always returned threefold.

Prayer and Mediation

In Chapter 1 we discussed the importance of living prayerfully, so it is not surprising to see that prayer and meditation are important components to a ritual's blood. Meditation helps you change your modes of thinking and brings the inner stillness necessary for communing with Spirit (see Chapter 4). Prayer then initiates contact, driven by intention and respectfulness.

Meditation usually precedes a ritual as a way of personal preparation. Prayers often come later, to greet or dismiss spiritual powers. Despite this generality, your prayers and meditations can come at any time and take any form with which you're comfortable and proficient.

Songs and Chanting

For the Aborigines, sacred songs and chants link them with the dreamtime of the Ancestors. Among the Navaho, intricate "chant ways" are part of healing rituals, each of which can take a lifetime to master. In Oceanic tradition, if one would know the truth, then sing! No matter the setting, ritual songs and chants express the shaman's intention and reverberate with power. Through the shaman's song all those listening experience magic in one form or another.

The most powerful ritual song you can use is one you make or find yourself (see Chapter 1, the section "A Shamanic Pathworking"). In this music that originates with your vital breath, everything you have been, are, and will be can find expression. This is so much the case that some Native Americans tell us that if you want to touch Spirit within and without, simply sing your personal song.

Even if you don't consider yourself much of a singer, you can make sacred sounds during your rituals to attract and release specific types of energy. The "oh," or "om" sound opens the self and draws the boundary of the sacred circle into your aura. An "ah" sound integrates and soothes. The "ee" sound is dynamic, motivating experience and transformation through growth. Mix and match the sounds with whatever comes from deep inside, and before you know it you have a personal sound that tunes you into the creative forces of all things.

Structures

Structures like the underground kiva of the Hopi, Zuni, and Pueblo, the sweat lodges of numerous traditions, and natural structures like caves all play an important symbolic and physical role in certain rituals. Each of these regions represents an inner sanctum of sorts, or an entrance to the lower realms for spirit travel. Here the shaman and/or the participants gather to transform like a butterfly emerging from a cocoon.

While building a kiva or moving a ritual to a cave isn't easy these days, it is still possible recreate the concept. For example, a dark curtain or tent might substitute for a cave of rebirth. A heavy blanket might be placed over someone to act as a temporary kiva within which he or she is left alone to contemplate Spirit. At many outdoor gatherings sweat lodges might be recreated in *very* simplified form using hot rocks and water. Indoors on a personal level, a steamy shower might substitute. The key here, again, isn't simply "ripping off" the tradition, but finding a meaningful way to adapt it considering your circumstances and aims.

Talking Stick

Each person who participates in a shamanic circle is valued and honored. The talking stick illustrates this by remaining available to all gathered. When one person has the talking stick, all others listen intently.

Usually the talking stick will be passed all around a circle and offered to everyone once during a gathering. As the stick reaches you, try not to worry about what you'll say. Just talk from your heart. The purpose of the talking stick is to encourage truthfulness and realness within your tribe.

☽

There are certainly more elements that could potentially be mingled with your ritual's blood, such as decorations and power objects. What is most important is that you listen to your heart when choosing and mixing the ritual together. Like baking a perfect cake, more isn't necessarily better here. A few well-chosen ingredients can create a work of perfection that you really get to enjoy because of the simplicity. So don't feel that incorporating each of these sample elements is necessary for a "good" ritual. The only real gauge as to what's "good" is what leaves you empowered afterward.

THE WHEEL OF TIME AND LIFE

> *To everything there is a season, and a time to*
> *every purpose under heaven.*
>
> —Ecclesiastes 3:1

Rituals celebrate or commemorate something, express a need, honor a cycle, or venerate the Divine. On a reoccurring basis, this creates an annual rhythm and spiritual coherency within which our inner shaman is fed and nurtured. More importantly, each ritual makes us stop for a moment and remember the Sacred, no matter what else has been happening, or where we may be. I strongly advocating having some type of rituals that you perform regularly as part of your shamanic quest.

Many New Age books have discussed the different types of rituals and given lengthy examples of each. In the interest of not repeating that work, what I'm providing here is a brief overview of various ritual themes and timing ideas instead of specifically outlined rites. As you begin practicing urban shamanism, you may want to include some of these timely themes into your tradition as schedules allow.

The Moon

As the only source of real light in the night sky, shamanic peoples often looked to the moon (and many parts of nature) for metaphoric symbols around which they constructed everyday life and rituals. The moon of each month received a name suited to the climate or culture of the tribe. This name described something in the earth's cycle or the people's tasks during that moon.

MOON NAMES FROM DIFFERENT SHAMANIC TRADITIONS

January	Wolf moon, frost moon, snow moon, manitou moon, quiet moon, chaste moon
February	Soft earth moon, light returns moon, starving moon, trapper's moon, cleansing moon
March	Storm moon, sap moon, fish moon, worm moon, flower time moon, seed and plow moon
April	Egg moon, planting moon, water moon, leaf spread moon, pink moon, budding tree moon
May	Milk moon, hare moon, ice melting moon, corn planting moon, dryad moon, joy moon

June	Strawberry moon, honey moon, hoeing corn moon, rose moon, lover's moon, fat moon
July	Buffalo breeding moon, raspberry moon, blessing moon, thunder moon, go home kachina moon
August	Grain moon, woodcutter's moon, gathering moon, mating moon, dispute moon, harvest moon
September	Hunter's moon, barley moon, spiderweb moon, little wind moon, wine moon, wood moon
October	Leaf falling moon, changing moon, sandstorm moon, basket moon, blood moon
November	Frosty moon, new snow moon, dead moon, ancestor's moon, deer shedding horns moon
December	Baby bear moon, oak moon, winter houses moon, cold month moon, wolf moon, long night moon

For the urban shaman, the moon's names and significance will likely change a lot. What I suggest is thinking about your annual sequences. What does each month represent in the natural order of your life? Or, spend a year noting what's going on during the full moon of each month. Find a short phrase to describe that activity and/or what energies you seem to need most, then apply that idea in your ritual construct.

To illustrate, my monthly moons go like this: staying in moon, birthday moon, melting moon, rain moon (or mud moon), bare feet moon, lawn cutting moon, barbecue moon, harvest garden moon, children to school moon, prepare house for winter moon, first snow moon, family and friends moon. Using this information in an annual ritual format isn't difficult. In January I stay indoors and focus my ritual efforts on looking within and integration. February is my birthday, so I have a birthday blessing ritual. March finds the snows beginning to melt in Buffalo, so I hold a ritual where I melt an ice cube, and also melt away the barriers in my heart.

Come April we get tons of rain, so I use rain water to sprinkle and purify the sacred space and/or dance in the rain as part of the rite. If it's really muddy, then I make mud packs or other healing salves out of the earth. By May, my children and I have shed our shoes and are reveling in the sun. This month's ritual theme is the air element and liberation. In June I have to start tending the lawn and landscaping, so this is my time for earth-centered rituals. In July I barbecue all month long as a type of fire festival, August represents an "in gathering" of first fruits, some of which become offerings, and September is a time to perform rituals for my children's well-being at school.

Closing out the year, the house has to be insulated in October against the cold. Ritually this is a time for protection. November usually brings the first snows, giving the earth some peace. I focus on similar goals and rest a bit before the holidays begin. Finally, December is a time for family and friends to gather and celebrate our tribe together.

Your lunar rituals will be far different from mine, but I think you'll find them very satisfying. You can always change the names and symbolic values for each month as you experience changes in your living environment and personal activities. This way your lunar rituals will always reflect who you've become as an individual, within your tribe, and as a spiritual being.

The Seasons

The wheel of time and life is forever moving, and the seasons potently represent that motion in nature's changes. The ancients had to pay close attention to this change in order to survive. They also believed deeply that each cycle, each season, had symbolic value to the spiritual seeker. So, they honored the turning wheel in annual ritual observances, hoping to give strength to the sun, to appease nature spirits, and to inspire personal growth. We can do likewise.

Nearly every metaphysical tradition has some form of seasonal rites. There is no reason not to follow yours as they stand, as long as they have meaning for you. If you don't already have a seasonal ritual calendar, or are looking for alternative themes for seasonal observances, consider these correspondences:

SPRING is the time of air, the winds, and new beginnings. Focus on clearing away the old (cleansing) and blessing new projects. Create and cultivate, be truthful and real. Use feathers, bells, and aromatics in your rituals to honor the wind.

SUMMER is the time of fire, the sun, and activity. Foster relationships and positive self-expression. Interact and savor, be present and attentive. Use incense, candles, and other fire sources in your rituals to honor the sun.

FALL is the time of water, coolness, and preparation. Honor the harvest, inspire wisdom, or direct your attention toward inner beauty. Give and receive, prayerfully and thankfully. Use seashells, dew, or tears to honor the water element.

WINTER is the time of earth, grounding, and rest. Invoke sacred dreams, encourage patience, and nourish the self. Share and renew through thoughtfulness and silence. Use seeds, soil, and potted plants to honor the earth element.

Seasonal themes often vary from tradition to tradition. For example, since winter is associated with the North, its alternative elemental correspondence is air in some shamanic settings. East's alternative element is fire, being the region of the rising sun, and south is sometimes associated with water and the season of spring instead of summer. These types of variations occurred due to the differences in climates and environmental logistics. Think about what each season represents to you elementally, where you would place it in the sacred wheel, and then make the appropriate adjustments in your ritual's themes and scheduling.

Rites of Passage

Life is full of change. Rites of passage mark those changes in a ritual setting to help with the integration process. Traditionally such rites were confined to birth, adulthood, eldership, and death. The creative urban shaman, however, has many more options available. Any significant change in your life can be honored and empowered through a rite of passage, including:

- Moving to a new residence
- Changing jobs
- Adoption
- Starting a new path
- Graduations
- Mastering a skill
- Recovery from extended illness
- Accomplishing a long-term goal
- New relationships
- Divorce
- Retirement
- Pregnancy
- Going to college
- Traveling abroad

Exactly what occurs in your rites of passage depends on the occasion and what it means to you. Someone celebrating the end of a long-term illness, for example, might use the passage ritual to symbolize a death to the old self and sickness, and a joyful rebirth. A pregnant woman might use the passage ritual to welcome the spirit of her unborn child, and to begin energizing herself for the new role of motherhood.

In this way, a rite of passage outwardly represents what has already occurred inwardly with self, your environment, the tribe, or the Sacred. It also prepares the way for what's yet to come. Considering our fast-paced society, this "time out" for recognition and reconnection becomes very important. Otherwise we can find ourselves waking up one day completely out of sync with the face staring back from the mirror. So stay alert to the ever-changing self, honor your passages, and ritually integrate them in meaningful ways as often as possible.

Communal, Tribal Transcendence

This type of ritual emphasizes human unity, and getting past the boundaries that keep people from being real with one another. I personally believe this tribal transcendence occurs most frequently in the confines of a ritual drumming circle. Dan Liss [danliss@mindspring.com], an ardent urban shaman, confirmed this theory recently. He described the experience of community drum circles by saying:

> I have been leading drumming circles for two years at a local metaphysical store. The participants' religious backgrounds vary drastically, ranging from Pagan to Jewish. Yet all seem to join their heart and spirit to the music. There's a sympathy in drumming, an energy that draws all people, helps them express natural spiritual empathy, and bridges the gaps that would otherwise separate Spirit from self, and person from person.

I have also seen the transcendence occur in Sufi dance circles, and in chanting circles where each person follows his or her inner voice in lending a sound or phrase to the echoes around him or her.

I remember one gathering in Pennsylvania with people from around the world. Many could not communicate with one another, and many spiritual paths were present. Even so, once the toning started you would have thought this group had practiced together for years! The resulting music was a vibrational experience in human unity that I find difficult to describe.

Many urban shamans have chosen a solitary path for spiritual expression, or been forced into it due to circumstances. Nonetheless, Dan's account and my personal experiences lead me to believe that communal workings are important to our development as people and a tribe. So, when opportunities present themselves, lend your voice, drum, or movements to that of a group gathered in mutual respect. Ritually celebrate the human tribe.

the sky kiva: the sacred space of home

These four walls provide a safe perch from which I can
contemplate all sorts of possibilities, knowing that on my
inner compass true north will always point me home.

—Linda Weltner, *No Place Like Home*

A kiva, in several North American tribes, is a sacred underground structure where many rituals traditionally begin or take place. Here, the spiritual fibers of tradition and myth are "fit together" for children and adults alike, then expressed through various observances. In an urban environment this process moves out from an underground structure into the sacred space of home, whether that "home" is a room or a whole house.

For shamans both past and present, whatever constitutes "home" also somehow reflects and incorporates the spiritual values of its inhabitants. Some tribes went so far as to represent the cosmos in a home's construction. This way, when gathered into the center of the dwelling, the family was truly living at the center of their universe. Other groups created round homes and insisted that the people within always move sunwise to keep the house filled with blessings.

These kinds of respectful expressions toward the home appear in traditions too numerous to mention. To me, this global correlation indicates that the special *feeling* of hearth and home is something the urban shaman should strive to create (or recreate). This chapter, therefore, discusses reclaiming the sanctity of your home by making your living space an expression of, and anchor for, your shamanic path.

Don't worry, this doesn't mean turning your life upside down or hiring interior decorators. Urban shamans are typically a practical lot. They know that reality doesn't come to a screeching halt when spiritual pursuits begin. Therefore, the advice given is here both mundane and metaphysical. This blend stimulates a meeting ground for Spirit with daily reality in the area where you spend most of your free time.

DECORATIONS

Home decorations give you the chance to symbolically surround yourself with Spirit in subtle ways. If these touches are blessed and energized, then the effect becomes more literal. Better still, since many decorations are a semi-permanent fixture in the home, they continue to radiate this energy, blessing everyone and everything in your living space.

In choosing, blessing, and placing decorative items for their symbolic value, follow the shamanic pattern created in Chapter 1:

1 *Think quietly* about what you want to represent and why, and then go looking for a suitable decorative item (or make it). While most of us don't have a lot of time for crafts these days, handmade items store more of your personal energy and reflect your creative vision. So if time allows, some kind of personal touch is advised, even if it's only putting a little polish or paint on a purchased item.

Remember that in choosing decorations, you don't have to forego utility. If, for example, you're hoping to banish negativity in your life and bring in more spiritual light, a well-chosen lamp or candle fixture might be a clever option. Or, if you want to surround yourself with nature but have a black thumb, use nature prints in curtains, tablecloths, rugs, placemats, and wallpaper instead.

2 *Pay attention* to Spirit's voice and your own intuition. Both will rarely lead you to something that's out of your budget's range, or inappropriate to your living space. While our society often subscribes to the "fancier is better" school of thought, the urban shaman knows better. Trappings mean little if there isn't substance behind them. Spirit and intuition seek out that substance.

To cite personal examples, over the last thirteen years, I only recall two occasions when I felt really drawn to an object that I wouldn't normally think of buying or taking home. The first time I found an incredible fox carving (the silver fox is one of my animal guides), but I just couldn't justify the cost. So, I asked Spirit to provide the money if it was meant to be mine. By the end of that day I'd made what I needed for household bills, plus just enough for the totem.

On the second occasion I saw a huge African drum. In a later conversation, I jokingly said that the universe would have to "drop it in my lap" because there was no way I could afford it or easily transport it. That very day a man offered to trade me the drum for $50 worth of my books (the value of the drum is easily seven times that)! Both of these examples show that when we're truly guided by the powers to something that seems impossible to obtain, Spirit will open the doors necessary to make it possible.

3 *Pray* over the right item once it is found, indicating in the prayer the token's purpose. Don't worry about your words. Focus on intention and communicating from your heart.

After praying, smudge the token with sage or another purifying herb. Take your time and don't skimp on this step. You don't want the object's vibrational value tainted by residual energies it picked up before it came into your hands. Just keep visualizing white light pouring into the object and continue smudging until you feel it's totally, psychically clear.

4 *Integrate* the item's function with a specific power phrase that will activate the energy and symbolism you've placed inside. To illustrate, say you buy a garlic braid for your kitchen as a symbol of health. Give the garlic braid an activating phrase like "be well" by whispering the phrase into the braid three times (once each for body, mind,

and spirit). These words carry healing power and saturate the garlic with your intention through vital breath and verbalization. Later, each time you think of it, say "be well" when you pass the garlic. This releases ongoing healthy energy to the area where you prepare food.

5 *Thank* Spirit for its help, and ask for continued blessings as you put the object in its new place of residence.

These steps may seem terribly simple, but they really make a difference in the way that you perceive your home. Everything around you holds the potential for magic if you just look with a creative eye, and anything can demonstrate your spiritual path if it's meaningful and treated respectfully. The following are three other specific examples of how decorative touches can reflect and energize your inner shaman.

Elemental Embellishment

A shaman looks at the world as having four quarters, each aligned with an element. The idea behind elemental embellishing is to find a way to represent these elements (earth, air, fire, or water) in the home by placing a symbolic token as closely as possible to a corresponding directional quarter. This way, the powers that make up nature and represent universal patterns will encircle you with protective, nurturing energy all the time. Additionally, these tokens create an informal sacred space that can be augmented when you invoke the quarters for ritual (see Chapter 2, "Ritual").

To accomplish the elemental scheme, you must first determine which direction you associate with each element. For example, someone with a fireplace in the north part of his or her home might use that as the "fire" quarter. Someone with a lake due north, might associate it with "water." Yet another person following Wiccan correspondences might associate the northern region with "earth." All approaches have merit (see Chapter 2). You just need to decide what makes the most sense, considering your space, personal vision, and path.

Next, find the northern part of your home. To figure this out, check a regional map, a survey, or use a compass. Make a mental note of this region of your living space so you know where to place objects later.

ELEMENTAL DECORATIONS OR ARCHITECTURAL REPRESENTATIVES

Earth	Potted plant, crystals, a globe, fresh flowers, wooden furniture or framing, mineral matter
Air	Wind chimes, an open window, gathered feathers, fans, aromatics, images of winged creatures
Fire	Candles, a fireplace, pilot light, hot spices, kindling, two-edged items
Water	Seashells, a pet's water dish, the bathtub/shower, hose, fish bowl, kelp, driftwood

AND, FOR IN-BETWEEN AREAS:

Earth/Air	Hanging plant, strings of drying herbs
Fire/Air	Incense, potpourri
Earth/Fire	Sand candle, sand or soil brazier, cactus
Earth/Water	Mud mask, fish tank with rocks
Water/Fire	A lava lamp, floating candles
Water/Air	A free-standing humidifier

Third, pick out, make, or designate appropriate items for each quarter. Please note that some suitable accessories or fixtures might already exist in the correct quarter of your home, such as a ceiling fan in the east for air. Don't overlook the obvious! Just because something's manmade doesn't eliminate its potential. In urban shamanism we seek to honor the sacredness inherent in all things. By giving manmade objects a *spiritual* place of honor and significance, we begin achieving that goal.

Move the chosen or created item to where it belongs, or mentally note the symbolism of any item that was already in place. As you do this, focus wholly on your intentions and the meaning of that object (possibly give it a power phrase as in step 4, above). For example, when your home seems physically and emotionally dry, placing a humidifier between the "water" and "air" quarter honors both those elements, negates the physical problem, and neatly generates fluid, motivating energy.

Similarly, when calling on the winds of change and incentive for a ritual, thoughtfully turn on a ceiling fan if a window isn't feasible! No matter the goal, remain consciously aware that the designated item is no longer just a decoration or an architectural fixture, but a purposeful representation of the life-giving powers of all creation.

Medicine Shields

Traditional medicine shields were often beautifully simple in design. For example, Crow Indians painted a war shield with concentric red circles and black dashes outside each circle. The red represented trouble, while the black dashes kept that trouble from escaping the shield. A warrior carrying this believed his or her enemies could not touch them.

Despite the name's implications and this particular example, medicine shields were used for far more than just healing or battle. The medicine shield represents its maker's spiritual life and goals, having often been fashioned with the help of a shaman. In this case, since we're becoming our own shaman, that assistance must come from within.

The purpose of a medicine shield is indicated by the symbols painted on it, and any attached trinkets. The power, however, comes from every part of the creation process and your personal resolve.

No matter how simple or complex the design, the assembly of your medicine shield must be a seriously considered project.

Start by asking yourself two important questions. First, what purpose will this shield fulfill when its done? Second, what symbols, colors, patterns, and power objects best represent this purpose? Gather together whatever you need to create those representations and objects. Cleanse and bless each using a sprinkling of saltwater or a smudge stick, then lay the shield's components on the floor in front of you along with whatever surface you've chosen for a base. (For craft instructions on making shields, see Chapter 9, the section on "Tools of the Trade.")

Close your eyes and breathe deeply while holding the shield's surface in both hands. Welcome the elements; honor the Sacred. Then, keeping your eyes closed, begin turning the shield clockwise until you feel that north is directly at the top. Place it down on the floor in that position and close your eyes again.

Visualize the shield as it lays on the floor. Using the paintbrush of your imagination, begin seeing the surface covered with the symbols, tokens, and/or patterns you've chosen in full color. This image might take a little while to form, so be patient with yourself. Most people are unaccustomed to using their imagination quite so vividly for a creative endeavor. Also know that the image might vary from what you originally anticipated. These variations come from your instincts and Spirit, so pay attention to any meanings they convey.

When you have the complete picture of the finished shield in mind, open your eyes and get to work! Let your hands be guided by the visualized portrait. As you work, recite the name of each symbol or pattern and its significance, to augment its purpose. Chant or hum a sacred song to increase the joyful, life-affirming energy that your shield absorbs. Finally, let the work set for twenty-four to forty-eight hours (for drying or whatever) and then put the shield in its intended location.

Tribal Helps and Hints

Here are some neat tips that I've collected from various urban people around the country who are part of my extended tribe. Each found a unique way to strengthen and inspire the inner shaman in every room of the home.

BEDROOM: Put glow-in-the-dark stars on the ceiling in an expanding pattern for growing consciousness. Add glitter to the ceiling paint to resemble the night sky. Wrap yourself in symbolically colored or patterned blankets so you can sleep surrounded by the vibrations you most need. (Note: Blankets like this are often available at museum and nature shops or native stores.) Put up posters that help you relax (or those suited to a goal) for pre-bed meditations. Hang a dream catcher over your bed (see Chapters 6 and 9) when seeking spiritual dreams.

BATHROOM: Paint affirmations around the mirror in calligraphy, and put a collection of spiritual books in a basket on the top of the toilet for undisturbed reading. Hang a decorative bundle of carefully chosen aromatic herbs in the shower. These release specific energies into your aura while you bathe. Leave flower-shaped aloe or heather-scented soap at the sink side to inspire inner beauty. Put out color-coded towels and washcloths depending on the vibrations needed each day.

DINING ROOM: Include a centerpiece that has space for a candle. Change the candle's color or scent to mirror your needs/goals. Light it as part of mealtime prayers. Pick out plates, cups, or other eating paraphernalia that have patterns accenting your goals. For example, use china with a fruit pattern to inspire "fruitfulness."

ENTRYWAY: Leave a wish bowl here filled with change. Anyone who contributes to the fund, makes a wish. People who need spare change may take of it, thereby spreading blessings. Hang bells (or chimes) outside the door or just over the doorway to chase away negativity. Affix small gargoyles to the staircase so they face different directions (alternatively, place them over doorways similarly). This protects your home from mal-intent.

FAMILY ROOM: Work some coriander into a heart-shaped wreath for this room to keep harmony in your family. Highlight the room with sky blue touches to accent tranquility and "clear sailing." Place freestanding citrine crystals in all four corners of the room for creative communication. Several families I know keep family altars here or an ever-burning candle to represent the family's spiritual unity.

KITCHEN: Put a photograph of every member of your household near the hearth (stove or microwave) to keep relationships warm. Hang up scented potholders with aromas and designs that symbolize your magical intentions. Choose trivets similarly. Place spiritual magnets (like the word sets) on the refrigerator to literally attract the energy they represent.

LIVING ROOM: Keep a green agate crystal ball (or other greenish brown stone) here to represent the Mother. Hang symbolic sun catchers in the windows or off of lamps to flood the room with harmonic light. Put small accent mirrors on the wall to reflect away unwanted energy. During the summer put up sheer curtains in different colors so the light that flows through accents your goals.

MEDITATION AREA: Use glow-in-the-dark string and pattern it like a web to represent life's network. Illuminate with candlelight. This is also an interesting component for making an illuminated dream catcher. Get an electric water fountain to honor the water element and use it as an effective stress reducer/meditative tool. In the fountain put tumbled stones with energies that mirror your needs (like amethyst for peace).

RECREATION ROOM: Use pseudo-grass to mimic the lawn, adding potted plants and trees around the room to improve the visual effect. Paint murals on the wall depicting the moon, sun, power animals, or other important personal symbols. Paint pool balls with runes or other magical sigils so that as you hit the balls, you release the energy they represent. "Pocketing" the ball aids with manifestation.

☾

It's quite likely that some of these ideas aren't suited to your living space. Even so, I hope that they inspire some creative notions of your own. As you can see, there are ways to modify even common games (like the pool table) so that they work in a spiritual construct. Just open yourself to the possibilities, and see what wonderful, whimsical ideas come up!

HOME AROMATHERAPY

Aromatherapy is a re-emerging art that allows us to bring a little bit of outdoors, indoors. Scents have a powerful impact on both the conscious and subconscious mind. To validate this truth for yourself, just wander past a bakery first thing in the morning and see what physical and emotional responses the aromas generate.

Early shaman-priests were likely aware of sensual influences when they put aromatic woods and spices into incense. These mixtures were burned for various purposes, including averting sickness, easing sadness, inspiring love, and purification. In modern times we've begun to recognize that many of the ancient aromatic formulas still hold merit, such as the use of sage for cleansing (chemically, sage has mild anti-bacterial qualities).

With this in mind, it is but a short jump forward to adapting and applying aromatic lore to our homes, and any other areas where we spend a lot of time, such as the office or in the car. Spread a ritually prepared tincture on window ledges to carry energy throughout a region with each breeze. Put a little blessed oil on lightbulbs, then turn on the lamp for active energy and manifestation. Sprinkle different symbolic scents in various rooms, depending on your needs and goals. Dab a little on yourself too!

Some of the correspondences I'm listing here do, indeed, come out of shamanic tradition (noted as such with an asterisk). The rest derive from associations that exist in similar spiritual settings, such as that of Wicca. I have, however, limited this list to items that can readily be found around the house, on supermarket shelves, or at nearby New Age stores to suit the urban shaman's hectic schedule.

AROMATIC CORRESPONDENCES

Anise	Increasing one's sensitivity to Spirit and the Astral reality. Cooking with it releases the aroma.
Apple	Happiness. Smell a fresh slice of apple whenever you need a little more joy. Burn dried apple rind to lift emotional heaviness throughout the home.
Basil	Peace and unity. The scent of basil promotes harmony between people.
Cedar	Safety. Place a piece of cedar wood in any area that needs protection, cleansing, or decreased negativity. Also, burn it as incense or use in potpourri.
Chamomile	Decreasing anger (try it as a tea). Or, sprinkle on your rugs to absorb ire, then vacuum it up, leaving behind only the aroma and its positive energy.
Chamomile	Relaxation. Use as suggested above.
Cinnamon	Power. Leave bundles of cinnamon sticks anywhere you want to draw more energy, passion, or good fortune. Sprinkle a bit in your shoes so its power walks with you.
Geranium	Balance, especially emotional. Add dried geranium petals to potpourri or incense. Or, steep fresh petals in apple juice to literally internalize their energy.
Ginger	Increasing memory retention. Add fresh ginger root to fried foods to release its aroma. Or, dab a bit of gin-

gered oil on your temples. (Warning: People with sensitive skin may find this harsh, so dilute it with almond or olive oil first.)

Grapefruit	Hopefulness. Cut open a grapefruit and sniff it when you're depressed, or drink a fresh glass of juice.
Jasmine	Improving self-image. Best burnt in incense.
Lavender✲	Improving sleep and peacefulness in any form.
Lemon	Purification. Try adding a little lemon juice to your household cleaning solutions. Look for lemon-scented air fresheners.
Marjoram	Easing anxiety. Since it comes in powdered form, this herb is easy to add to homemade incense (see recipe in Chapter 9).
Mint	Memory retention, avoiding mental tensions, and improving your ability to cope with financial difficulty. Pinch a fresh leaf to release its aroma or prepare dried mint in a tea or incense.
Mint✲	Decreasing restlessness. Prepare as above.
Nutmeg	Spiritual focus and psychics. An excellent aromatic for the meditation or ritual area.
Orange	Physical and spiritual tonic. Keep dried rinds to use in aromatic blends, or enjoy the aroma of a freshly cut orange at breakfast. Also augments devotion.
Pine✲	Cleansing and blessing. Readily available in cleaning solutions and air fresheners, but a natural blend is best if possible.
Rose	Encouraging love (including self love) and tranquility. Bring fresh roses into the house to attract love. Use rosewater in cooking to internalize self-love. For the whole-house effect, air fresheners and incense are often available in rose.

Rosemary	Memory retention. Also stimulates vitality, and has anti-depressant qualities. Fresh rosemary is best for all these purposes. Simply break the rosemary leaf to release its scent. Rub it on surfaces where you want the vibrations to stay.
Sage*	Purification and healing; overcoming depression.
Sandalwood	Psychism and healing. Try sandalwood powder as a base to your homemade incense.
Vanilla	Inspiring love and passion. All forms are fine.
Wintergreen*	Motivating youthful outlooks and energy. Best results come from the fresh leaves.

To my thinking, the best part about aromatic spiritual approaches is the subtlety. While you might be strongly aware of an aromatic at first, it slowly blends itself into the ambiance of your home, silently releasing its power. No one will think you odd for scenting your living space, or for wearing a unique perfume. Better still, since aromatics float on the winds, our choices have the potential of blessing many people who come near or into our sacred spaces.

HOUSE BLESSINGS

Beauty extends from the fireside of my hogan.
—Navajo house blessing song

While many people only perform house blessings when they move into a new home, this can become an ongoing mini-ritual that you enact every day through thoughtful actions. For example, each day get up and light a candle to honor your house Spirit. Greet that energy warmly, and ask the Great Spirit to continue the blessings in your home before rushing off to work.

Set up some type of semi-permanent personal or family altar where aspects of your faith can remain as ongoing reminders of the

Sacred. Anoint your home with empowering oils and chant sacred songs while you straighten up at the end of the day. In whatever forms possible, turn away the business, noise, and harshness of urbania from your personal space so that it truly remains a sanctuary.

On those occasions when you want something more formalized than what daily maintenance provides, try this house blessing ritual. I've kept it brief so that it can easily be slipped into nearly any day's routine, but you can certainly expand it. Read through the ritual a couple of times. Meditate about it and about what your home means to you, then make any personal changes desired. This takes a little more time than just using the prefabricated rite, but it will make the effort far more meaningful, and therefore more successful.

House Blessing Ritual

INVOCATION: If you have a family or personal altar set up, start the invocation there; otherwise, begin in the room where you spend the most time. Invite the Great Spirit and the elemental powers into your home in any way that feels comfortable. Make known your intentions, and ask for their assistance in making your entire living space into a haven that defends and supports your inner shaman.

PRAYER: Recite this prayer or another of your choosing while moving clockwise around your home. This motion inspires blessings. Repeat the prayer as many times as necessary to complete a full circuit of your home, stopping in each room (don't forget the cellar, attic, and/or garage). Take some burning sage, sweetgrass, or lavender with you to banish residual negativity.

> *Sun Father, shine in my home. Let me see clearly, and begin each day in this sacred space with hope. Earth Mother, give my home firm foundations. Let me and mine grow strong here together. Brother Air, move ever through my home with inspiring winds. Let me breathe of your inspiration and clarity daily. Sister Sea, wash through this place with healing waves. To each day bring a fullness of emotions and peace.*

ACTIVITIES: In the center of the home, preferably close to your fireplace or stove, light a candle saying:

This candle represents the spirit of my home and all who live or visit here. By the blessings of Spirit and the Ancestors, may it always be filled with perfect love, truth, peace, harmony, and wholeness.

Let this candle burn in a safe place, replacing it as necessary. If leaving a candle burning twenty-four hours a day seven days a week isn't feasible, leave on any light source to represent ongoing warmth and health in your home.

It is appropriate at this point to leave out a small gift of food for the people in your tribe who have passed over. This symbolically welcomes their presence as guiding, protective powers in your home. Put the food where it can remain undisturbed for twenty-four hours, then give it to animals or compost it so that the blessings continue to flow from that offering.

CLOSING: Dismiss the guardians in any way you wish. Thank them for coming, and ask that they continue to watch over your home and fill it with love. If possible, spend the remainder of your day puttering around your house. Let your inner shaman revel in spiritual safety. Enjoy the clean, energized space you've created with Spirit's help.

PROTECTION

House blessings help to keep your living space safe from unwanted energy. Even so, those of us who live in urban environments are often barraged by "bad vibes." People are carrying a lot of tension and emotional baggage these days, and in the city there are *lots* of people. The geometric effect this can have on one's living space can best be explained through a personal example.

I was living in a heavily populated, somewhat rough neighborhood in Boston, Massachusetts about thirteen years ago. After a couple of months I noticed that all kinds of problems were happening to me every day, both inside and outside my house…appliances malfunctioned, pets got sick, the car broke down regularly, items were being misplaced, and the like. It seemed almost as if trouble was following me, and every night I found myself with a throbbing headache that refused to go away.

Finally, when I could stand no more, I called a Wiccan friend who almost immediately asked me if I'd ever put any type of psychic protection on my home or vehicle. At that time, I didn't even know what psychic protection was, so she kindly offered to come over and help. Afterward, the change in the apartment was almost audible. My headaches went away, and the daily difficulties faded. My home just needed some astral reinforcement, and yours might too.

There are any number of metaphysical techniques you can use to put up protection. Visualization seems among the most popular for urban shamans, along with the use of protective anointing oils and specially prepared amulets. In visualization, the idea is to draw protective energy into yourself, and then channel it outward to every corner of your home. As you imagine this, it helps to see a mirrored sphere or something similar that extends beyond the physical into the astral. (Note: This is *very* important, since shamans travel the astral regularly.) The mirrored exterior reflects away unwanted or mal-intended energy, and surrounds you in three-dimensional protection.

This imagery doesn't work for everyone, so find something that makes you feel safe. One friend visualizes her childhood blanket wrapping her living space, while another puts up astral classical art on the walls, believing that "evil" cannot withstand the face of beauty. Both approaches have tremendous merit, and show just how creative you can be with your visualization if you choose.

A second method uses the vibrations in specially prepared oils to keep unwanted energies at bay, or to reinforce protective wards that are already in place. The additional benefit of this approach is the subtle aromatherapy impact. This gives everyone entering your home a sense of comfort. I call this the "ahh" effect. Visitors sit down and almost immediately relax, subconsciously knowing they're sheltered somehow from the outside world.

To make such an oil for yourself, begin with a base of good olive oil. During a full moon (for thorough protection) warm one cup oil with one teaspoon of any (or all) of the following protective herbs:

myrrh	sandalwood	anise	basil
rosemary	bay	cinnamon	dill
fennel	heather	lavender	sage
marigold	mint	pine	rose

Let the herbs steep in the oil until it smells strongly of them, then strain and keep in a dark, airtight container for use. If you wish, leave this container in the light of a noonday sun for an hour or so (to banish darkness). Then, whenever you feel your protection needs a little reinforcement, dab this on every door, window, and other openings in your home. This symbolically closes the "open paths" into your house to all but those spirits and energies you wish.

A third approach is the use of specially prepared, and carefully placed household amulets. By definition an amulet is a preventative; it protects you against malevolent intentions and danger. Ancient shamans often used precious stones, metal, or plants as amulets. All of these options hold potential if you can keep the chosen amulet from being handled or otherwise disturbed once it is created.

I personally recommend an Eastern shamanic approach that uses mirrors or any highly polished surface as amulets. Begin by getting four small mirrors (one for each quarter of your home). Next, take a little of the protective oil that you made on the pointer finger of your strong hand. Trace a counterclockwise, concentric circle from the perimeter of each mirror into its center point saying,

Absorbed within, all evil, all din. Reflect away from me, all negativity.

Keep repeating this phrase until you reach the center point, then draw your finger directly up off the mirror's surface. Put these facing *outward* in the four directional regions of your living space. This way, the mirror doesn't take up excess space, and its surface is poised to collect or turn away unwanted energies from all directions.

By the way, if you don't like looking at the back of the mirror, decorate it with some paint, silk flowers, or whatever. Also, if you don't have enough wall or window space for four mirrors, try placing one on the floor face down (where you won't walk on it) and one on the ceiling face up. This creates the top and bottom point for your visualized mirror-bubble, and it also symbolizes the rede of "As above, so below."

These three illustrations confirm that spiritual safety measures don't have to be overly time-consuming, or take up a lot of space. Use these ideas as a place to start if you don't have any way of presently safeguarding your home. If, however, there are other methods of household protection that you enjoy or prefer, by all means use them!

What's most important here is keeping the protective energy in your living space constant. When this protective power lapses, you'll notice it, often through unpleasant events or increasing tension levels. So keep your spiritual eyes and ears alert. When life begins beating down the shield you've put in place, reinforce or rebuild it. Remember: The urban shaman's home is his or her spiritual castle. Nothing in this world or the next has the right to impose on that sanctuary without your permission.

MAINTAINING SACRED SPACE

A [sacred] space [is one] in which stillness can
be assured; a space to reflect, to study, or simply
to be alone.

—Mary Anthony Wagner

Even if you live alone there will be times when your sacred space of home gets disrupted. You know instinctively when this happens. It is those times when you feel awkward sitting in your own living room, as if something doesn't "fit" anymore. That something is the energy that caused the disruption in the first place.

Even the most adept shaman experiences this phenomena periodically. It's what I call psychic seepage. Somehow, a stray piece of warped energy or something else oozes through the shields you've put in place, most likely at a time when you were sick, weary, or out of sorts. These physical and emotional conditions create situations where your ability to detect weaknesses in, and physically maintain, your shields is severely hampered. When you recover, suddenly you discover the leak and need to stop it up. Before you do, however, take the time to get rid of the seepage with a thorough house cleansing. This way the residue won't be trapped inside the wards you're replacing.

House Cleansing

In much the same way that dust accumulates on your tables and shelves, psychic "dust" clings to everything in and around your home. This dust isn't just generated by you. It can come from psychic seepage, others who live in the house, a friend who unwittingly dumps emotional garbage on your doorstep, tensions in the neighborhood, and stress in the city itself. At regular intervals this muck and grime needs to be cleaned away.

You can accomplish this psychic housecleaning very easily through regular acts of maintenance. Whenever you notice psychic clutter, pick up the house. The very act of straightening is a renewal process filled with ritualistic overtones. As you go about your routine, the energy generated puts your home's ambiance back in order and restores the balance. This doesn't mean everything has to look like a photograph from *Better Homes and Gardens*; just gather up clutter on the floor and put anything that looks out of place back in its niche.

While you work, consciously pour positive energy through your hands into everything you touch. Visualize your cleaning rag collecting unwanted energy along with the dust, then neatly toss it outside. Or add purifying herbs, like a little lemon juice, to your wash water, and likewise toss that away outdoors (this symbolizes putting the unwanted energy away from you). Afterward, a good smudging of the home, frequently handled objects, and yourself should complete the effect.

A novel approach that I learned from another urban shaman uses a magnet. While my friend cleans up, he keeps a special magnet in his pocket. This magnet has been blessed and charged to "attract" psychic dirt. Afterward, he either soaks the magnet in saltwater to dispel the energy it collected, or if things were really bad, he ritually disposes of it.

When you're really pressed for time, try opening the curtains and windows throughout your living space at the first sign of dawn instead of cleaning up. Drawing back the curtains brings in daylight, which drives away any lingering shadows. Opening the windows lets the winds of change bring a fresh, revitalizing air to the entire space. If it is safe to do so, leave the house open like this until the sun sets. Otherwise, leave the windows open as long as possible, so the air has a chance to circulate completely.

Privacy Power

Besides having a psychically clean living space, sometimes our inner shamans need privacy: time to be alone with our thoughts and the Sacred. My home seems to have an ever-revolving door, so I know how difficult achieving these private moments can be. Besides turning off your phone, telling well-meaning friends to stay away, and putting up "Do not disturb" signs, how does one encourage spiritual solitude?

Bits of ancient folklore have ideas on this subject. Celtic shamans might sprinkle salt around an area they wanted left undisturbed, or wished to protect. In the United States this translated into putting a pinch of salt under the chair of an unwanted guest to get him or her to leave! In both cases, however, salt has what I call "keep away" power. Put some on your entryway when you need to be left alone. Basil leaves or patchouli oil are good alternatives.

Another option is having a specially blessed fern plant in your home. Plant the fern in a pot with a piece of paper upon which you've written the word "privacy." Include a small jet stone in the bottom of the pot too. This represents your firm resolve to find quiet shelter. Pray over the plant each time you water it, asking Spirit to energize it with the protective power of solitude.

Whenever you want to be ensured of privacy, purposefully put the fern in the front window or some other noticeable spot. From this defensive perch, the fern radiates protective, private energies. Also (on a practical level) let your friends and relatives know what this signal means. When you're ready to receive guests again, put the fern away to likewise "put away" its protective energy until needed again.

Reclaiming Space

Our society has become very mobile, as people are regularly moving out of one residence into another. As this shift occurs, the energy of both homes involved also changes, often becoming chaotic and unpredictable. I see this evidenced especially in college settings where roommates vary from year to year. The transitions happen so quickly that the energy of the living space never has a chance to settle down.

When you discover situations like this happening to you, and your living space seems psychically topsy-turvy, it is time to reclaim your space. The way to approach this problem depends heavily on the circumstances. For example, whenever I had a change of roommates, I found myself scrubbing and cleaning, moving furniture, putting up new posters, smudging, and the like. Basically my actions put *me*, and something of my inner shaman, back into that living space.

This kind of mini-ritual also works very effectively for those times when you feel like guests have irreverently trampled all over your personal space. By changing the physical patterns within the home, you alter the energy. This breaks any negative lines left by inconsiderate guests, and builds whatever new pattern you desire in its place. Your new design, whether the changes are large or small, kindles the reclaiming process. Don't forget to do a cleansing first, however. You will find that the overall effect is much more beneficial.

When you leave one home for another, the process is a little different. First, try to do a little spiritual housecleaning in your old home before you go. This helps break the ties between yourself and the space, and leaves behind a neutral energy zone for the new residents. A good way to accomplish this is by leaving your house candle (or lamp) burning until the very last minute. Carry this to the door with you, still lit. Then when leaving for the last time, blow out the candle, say good-bye, and release the house spirit. Leave the candle *inside* the door for the next resident(s) to find. If you don't feel that this is appropriate, just ritually dispose of it and get a new one for your new home.

If you don't have a house candle, then remain consciously aware of removing yourself from the old home one piece at a time with every item of furniture, clothing, art, and rug. Sprinkle a little salt on the floors before you go, then sweep up any remaining bits of yourself or your family's ties to this place and take them outside. Lock the door, and dispose of the salt.

For your new residence, always begin with a good house cleansing. Just because you're conscientious about spiritual housecleaning doesn't mean the former residents were. If these walls are talking, listen to what they have to say so that you know what remnants you're dealing with, and then clear away the chatter spiritually.

When you start moving in, light the house candle or lamp immediately. This acts like a letter of introduction to the house spirit (also sometimes called the hearth god or goddess). Then, as you put all your goods where they belong, you slowly build your energy into the new home and claim it as your own. Follow this with a house blessing.

Peace Pipe

One of the most disruptive emotions in any home is anger. This feeling taints the air throughout a living space until the situation is resolved. Even then, residuals can linger. To inspire forgiveness and begin dispelling the negativity, you might want to try this adaptation of a peace pipe ritual.

To begin, each person involved sits in a circle so that everyone is on equal footing. Before the ritual, you should not consume any alcohol for four days. This acts as a kind of offering that keeps body and intention pure.

In the center of the circle burn some sweetgrass to invite and please the spirits. In another bowl light some tobacco leaves (*not* a cigarette). This needs to be organic tobacco, if possible. Otherwise use an herb that represents peace to all those gathered.

The bowl of burning herbs should be passed to each member of the circle (with a potholder or other heat safety). As it reaches a person, accepting the bowl is a kind of sacrament. It represents a heartfelt promise to leave the past behind and move forward from this point.

With the bowl in hand, each participant raises it to the sky and down toward the ground to acknowledge the Creator and creation. This invites these two powers to bear witness to his or her promise. The individual should then proceed to pray for the ability to forgive, and offer forgiveness to all those gathered. From this moment forward the situation is "dead" and should not be discussed again without the consent of all those gathered.

Afterward, everyone should go through the house together, taking turns smudging various rooms with sweetgrass. This way everyone takes part in, and remains responsible for, maintaining the home's sanctity.

Musical Moods

Filling your home with music is one way to change its vibrations dramatically. Thankfully, there are many excellent artists whose work not only uplifts but also focuses our attention on the shamanic being we're striving to become. Here is a list of some of my personal favorite music for inspiring and rejuvenating the inner shaman:

- *Where Earth Touches the Stars*, The Ancient Brotherhood, distributed by Audio Alternatives (914-238-5943). Western shamanic focus.

- *World Visions*, The Rhythms, Global Pacific Music. Global shamanic rhythms.

- *At the Edge*, Mickey Hart, 360 Productions. Global shamanic rhythms. Also: *Planet Drum*.

- *Earth Quest*, Richard Searles, Earth Dance Music. Sounds to connect with the mythical, magical earth.

- *Quiet Heart, Spirit Wind*, Richard Warner, Enso records. Eastern shamanism.

The best part about music is that it truly is a universal language that speaks volumes to anyone who listens. This is one way to gently share your path with everyone who comes to your home. Additionally, you'll find music to be a great helpmate in shamanic journeys. The sounds, vibrations, and words can transport your spirit back to the world tree to transcend everyday reality and reconnect with both the Sacred, and the shaman within.

shamanic journeying

*Don't tell me about your visions
unless they grow corn.*

—Sun Bear, Chippewa medicine man

At home or away, trance work is an essential element to nearly all shamanic rituals and magic. A shaman uses a trance state to access and travel the world tree (or something similar). He or she also uses it as a means of seeking out appropriate spirits for information and insight.

This chapter reviews the fundamentals of shamanic trance work. It discusses why and how you can use this methodology for astral travel and gaining insights from a variety of spiritual entities. For those who feel somewhat uneasy about this, shamanic journeying bears no similarity to necromancy. Instead of bringing a spirit into the temporal, the shaman goes to Spirit and gets information directly. The shaman always remains in control of this encounter, and can disengage himself or herself at any time. And, while an adept shaman might choose to allow spiritual possession for divination or another important purpose, this is always a choice, not a requisite.

MEDITATION

If you haven't done so already, developing effective meditation skills is the first step to successful trance work and shamanic journeying. Since the shaman believes the world to be what he or she *thinks* it is, the true power of meditation becomes clear. Your life's experience and your spiritual pursuits will be dramatically influenced by how you perceive them in a meditative state. Meditation also gives you a method and opportunity through which you can transform any imagery into something positive and life-affirming, including urbania.

Meditation means *the act of measuring*. During a meditation you heighten your ability to remain alert and aware of but one thing, instead of the hundreds of things your mind usually tackles. Through sustained focus on that situation, object, or idea, you "measure it up," as if turning it over and seeing it from different angles. From this perspective, you can then subsequently direct energy toward supporting that image, changing it, or banishing it altogether.

Some people feel daunted by nearly any procedure that has mystical overtones, but meditation is very user-friendly. In fact, you already experience light meditative states whenever you sit quietly and consider a topic, when you focus intently on a project, or concentrate completely on a work-related issue. You can recognize these moments fairly easily. The world around you seems to recede, and nothing exists but the matter at hand. If someone walks up to you and starts talking, it takes a while for you to recognize his or her presence, and even longer to snap back so that you can respond.

The difference between this experience and meditation as a spiritual practice comes down to conscious awareness, intention, and focus. Now instead of unwittingly drifting into a meditative state, you will consciously create it with an intention in mind. This intention remains as a focal point throughout the meditation. Please note that your meditative purposes don't have to be grand. Actually, one of meditation's most effective applications returns us to the sacred circle's beginning: taking time for thoughtfulness and stillness.

Breath

Nearly all spiritual traditions use controlled breathing as part of meditation exercises. Why? Because each part of a breath has physical, emotional, and spiritual effects that can encourage altered states of awareness.

Inhaling is an act of acceptance and renewal. Each new breath helps us to live presently, as a participant in our own destiny. Exhaling is an act of relief, release, and reception. When tension abates, you exhale a sigh. When you feel liberated, you sigh. As a truth is accepted, it's natural to exhale.

Between these two points comes stillness. Just like the moment between darkness and dawn, this instant poises between the worlds of action and waiting. The longer and smoother the pause, the deeper the meditative state, and the greater the chance of moving beyond meditation into a trance.

So, when you begin practicing meditation (any art requires practice to master it), you'll start by focusing on your breath. Take three deep, cleansing breaths at first, in through your nose and out through your mouth. Let your lungs fill completely from the bottom up, then release the air and relax. Consciously experience the full cycle of acceptance, stillness, and release.

With each breath let a little more tension float away as you exhale. Close your eyes. You need not see the outside world any longer. Direct your attention within. Find that private place inside known only to you and abide there with your breath and the beating of your heart.

Continue to breathe deeply in an all-connected manner until you no longer notice the transition from inhale, to pause, to exhale. This type of breathing symbolizes the sacred circle of life, and the natural order of things. It will naturally quiet your body and mind, and begin releasing your spiritual insights so they can function fully. Once you reach this point, you can begin "measuring" whatever you came here to evaluate.

Posture

The positioning of your body dramatically influences how you feel, think, and respond. This is not only because of the physical effects of a specific position, but also because of its symbolic pattern. As spiritual seekers we've come to understand that patterns are like blueprints for accessing and releasing energy. By placing one's body in a specific posture (e.g., the pattern), you open various chakras and create a line through which specific vibrations can subsequently flow.

Shamans understand this, and sometimes use physical postures to emphasize meditative focuses. For example, a warrior might stand in meditation when preparing for battle, so he or she is postured at-the-ready. Someone who is present and attentive, who is ready to act, usually isn't sitting down comfortably. Conversely, a lying posture emphasizes healing, receptivity, and tremendous respect. We lie down to rest and recuperate. Children often naturally lie down on their bellies to listen to stories. In some religions, lying before the altar represents humility and reverence.

Sitting meditations stress patience, observation, listening, information gathering, and the wisdom of letting things and people follow their own paths and power. For at least twelve years of our lives we sit in classrooms to learn, both from a designated instructor and from each other. Someone wishing to become a Buddhist monk often sits cross-legged before his or her teacher, or before the classroom of nature, listening and observing. When we realize the best thing we can do in a situation is nothing, we sit and watch.

Moving meditations, like those sometimes experienced on long walks, while cooking, or during other activities, are real timesavers, so they're perfect for urban shamans. Moving meditations augment creative problem solving, manifestation through action, and what I call natural "mulling." This is where we become so engrossed in a pattern of motion that it creates an altered state. During this time our mind chews up a lot of the information it has gathered and prepares to consume it or spit it out, depending on its quality and usefulness.

I should note at this point that posturing is an option, not a necessity, especially when limiting physical conditions exist. For example, I have ongoing severe back pain. Lying meditations ease that pain, but the discomfort from standing or sitting far outweighs the benefit of those postures, because it distracts me. I can't focus on spiritual matters when my body's yelling that loudly!

Additionally, some situations simply don't lend themselves to posturing. It's usually considered bad form to lie down on the job, for example. So, my advice is to try various postures in your home meditations to see how they make you feel, and how effective the results seem to be. If you find that a specific position improves your focus, then make note of it and use it whenever possible. Otherwise, place yourself in any posture that seems to make sense, considering the present circumstances.

Visualization

A third element frequently added to breath and posturing is visualization. Here you create a mental landscape that holds your attention focused on the meditation's goal, and also helps to manifest that goal. We often forget the power our imagination has for exhibiting real, quantifiable results. Artists, for example, "see" or "hear" something in their mind's eye, then create it through a medium so everyone can enjoy it. The goal of visualization is to create positive images (again, a pattern) through which manifestation can easily flow.

Effective visualization requires that you choose a motif that literally or symbolically represents your focus. The first symbol or scene that comes to mind is usually right on, so trust your instincts on this. If you can't come up with any ideas, try leafing through a book of symbols, dream dictionaries, or even a fully illustrated magazine, and see if anything makes sense. As you search, remember that visualizations don't have to be complicated, just meaningful. Simpler landscapes free your mind to focus more energy on experiencing and integrating. Also, people who have trouble with visualization need to begin with simple, forthright pictures until their skills improve.

During the meditation, wait to begin your visualization until after cyclic breathing has left you relaxed and centered. In some meditations you'll want the imagery to remain the same throughout, such as an empowering symbol for ongoing health. In other meditations you'll want to let the images evolve and transform, such as when you're trying to get an alternative perspective on a pressing problem. In both cases, however, the more three-dimensional and real the imagery becomes for you, the better the results will be.

Other Accents

For individuals who are experiencing problems meditating, or those who want more sensory input to help deepen meditative states, several other options exist. Here are just a few to try:

- Take a long bath or shower before meditation to decrease your tension levels.

- Play a relaxing instrumental tape, especially one with drumming.

- Burn incense suited to your goals. Sandalwood is a good all-purpose meditation incense, as is lotus.

- Wear special clothing, preferably nonconstraining.

- Light candles whose colors represent your goal. Or use a plain white candle to represent protection, peace, and the presence of Spirit. Dab an appropriate aromatic oil on the candle to further support the meditation's focus.

- Sit on an aromatic pillow (an aroma like lavender improves peacefulness).

- Go to a location in nature where you won't readily be disturbed, and where the Mother's voice can guide you.

☾

Whatever elements you've added to your meditative practices, once you've reached a comfortable level of awareness, simply let yourself *be*. Watch, listen, feel, relax, accept, and *be*. Don't try to create any particular outcome. Let things flow naturally. Throughout the process you may experience some odd sensations like floating, tingling, a light touch of air. Try not to let these sensations distract you. They're a natural outcome that occurs when your energy centers start to clear and open.

Also, don't worry about how long you are meditating. When you feel done, stop and make notes of the experience. For trance work, you'll want to slowly increase the length of time during which you can maintain a meditative state, but don't try and master it overnight. Effective meditation takes time, practice, and patience. Your tenacity will eventually pay off by pushing past any barriers that hold back your progress.

Over time, you'll also find it gets easier to meditate nearly anytime, anywhere. Stressed out at work? Take a fifteen-minute break in the lavatory and meditate! Need to tone down the noise around you at a hotel? Listen to your breath instead and meditate! These kinds of benefits are even more important for the urban shaman, allowing him or her to dramatically decrease daily anxiety levels while regularly increasing awareness.

TRANCE WORK

Trance work releases the human spirit from temporal perceptions. Because of the spiritual freedom a trance offers, a shaman uses this state to transcend his or her normal way of knowing and understanding, and we will be doing likewise. In entering a trance, you'll move beyond normal time-space constraints into a sphere of potentialities, possibilities, and psychic objectivity.

Trance work differs from meditation in intensity and magnitude. Meditation begins with discipline and focus. Trance work begins with meditation, goes to a much deeper level of awareness, and then becomes an exercise in letting go and experiencing the self outside of normal boundaries. To quantify this distinction, your average meditation session doesn't result in channeling, communion with Higher Powers, or astral travel. If any of these things occur, you have likely experienced a trance.

Trance work begins like a normal meditation exercise with breathing, sometimes combined with visualization. Some people also create sacred space at the outset of a trance, especially if they plan on meeting spirits during their travels. Like an insulating bubble of protective power, the sacred space safeguards the shaman against unwanted interference from other entities that exist in the astral landscape, and also keeps his or her spirit from wandering too far off track.

As with a meditation, you can add drumming, incense, background music, and any other sensual cues that turn your attention away from temporal thoughts toward Spirit. Unlike meditation, however, a trance state is rarely instantaneous unless you're very adept. Most people find it takes twenty to thirty minutes of deep meditation to reach a solid trance state, so don't expect immediate results and make sure you give yourself plenty of private time.

Your Shaman's Song
One thing that really helps activate a trance state is humming, chanting, or singing your shaman's song. By its nature, this song is designed to transport you to deeper levels of *being*. Let the vibrations linger on each breath you take. Feel them fill you and hold you.

As you hum or sing, you'll find that the song may start to vary from what you received in the pathworking (see Chapter 1). Let this happen naturally; don't fight it. Your power song is like the base note to a great symphony that exists in all creation, sometimes called the music of the spheres. Since life is ever-changing, this music also transforms, in this case to mirror the focus of your efforts. A song that takes you into a healing trance, for example, will differ from the one that sings you into a trance for spirit communication. Over time and practice, you'll remember each variation and be able to use the new songs for whatever journeys you undertake.

For those who must practice trance work in an environment unsuited to open singing or chanting, you can recite your shaman's song inwardly. Thoughts have just as much power (if not more) than verbalizations, so don't let your location hinder you. Turn your attention within, and sing from your soul.

Astral Entryways

You'll know that you're reaching deeper levels of awareness when you either no longer sense the physical whatsoever, you feel as if your body's floating or very heavy, or you experience sensations like those that occur just prior to falling asleep. For me, the physical sensation is fuzzy or tingly, and my ears start to buzz. Between breaths, in the moment of expectation, I start the journey that returns to the world tree explored in Chapter 1.

You, however, may find other entrances to the astral worlds more suited to your understanding. For example, some people climb a rope, ascend cloud-covered stairs, or take an elevator to the higher realms. Others travel down a well, on a subway, or through a tunnel to the lower realms. Still others might follow the roots of the world tree, open a door, emerge from a cave, or part a veil to enter the middle realms. Use whatever imagery seems right to you, but use it consistently.

Establishing a recognizable pattern into and out of each realm has two important benefits. It makes shamanic journeying far less taxing and much safer. The astral landscape can become quite distracting, or shift if other entities arrive. By regularly following the same imagery and routes, distractions and changes won't throw you off. You'll instinctively *know* the right paths for your journey and you'll be able to continue your work uninterrupted.

The Journey Home

Once your astral tasks are completed (this chapter will show you several examples), carefully follow the same pattern and imagery by which you came to go back again. Return to the entryway established for this realm. As you exit, do not allow for any tag-alongs. These are spirits who may try to follow after you, yearning for any type of companionship, or hoping to enter the earth-plane before their time. Simply turn and command the tag-along to stay back. This is your sacred space and your path to power. You have the right and the wherewithal to refuse unwanted or inappropriate advances or intrusions.

After the entry closes behind you, your body and senses will start returning to normal. Take your time adjusting to this change. Never move quickly after trance work; it causes a bad headache. Some people also find themselves quite dizzy after a deep trance, so standing up right away isn't advisable. Sit quietly for a few minutes, and have some raw vegetables or other healthy finger foods handy. These will help ground you and bring your body back to normal functioning levels. A tall glass of cold water also seems to smooth the transition process. By the way, I don't recommend consuming any sweets, caffeine, or alcohol for several hours afterward. Their effects seem far more drastic than usual during this interval.

Finally, always take the time to record or write out your experience. These notes will help you gauge your progress, successes, and failures, and they prove very helpful in considering future attempts.

Additionally, the information gathered during trance work has a timeless appeal. When you review these notes in the days and years ahead you'll find they have more insights to share with your growing spirit.

NAME QUESTS

> *Once you are real you cannot be ugly, except to*
> *people who don't understand.*
>
> —Marjorie Williams

Names have power. Ancient shamans acted on this maxim regularly. A sickly child's name might have been changed by the village shaman in order to fool or discourage the spirit of death. Or, a shaman might travel to the astral to learn the true name of a sickness's spirit, which then secured power over that spirit and helped to banish it. Just speaking the correct name of a spirit or fearsome animal was considered a type of invoking prayer that required an answer.

This reverence toward names resulted in tribal peoples often bearing multiple names, each one of which had special significance. One name might reflect a noble task or societal position. Another might be given after a long illness to represent a new life. Remnants of such naming customs still exist in our society, although much of the significance and power in them has been lost.

Your True Name

Based on the belief that a person's name(s) can dramatically affect him or her, the name quest seeks to uncover a person's true name, known only to him or her and the gods. Discovering your true name helps unlock the secrets of past lives, present psychic gifts, and your future potential. This name, sometimes called a soul name, will be something you can use in chanting or mantras for personal empowerment. It is also something you can use in identifying yourself to the guardians on the astral plane, who sometimes issue challenges to a seeker.

To discover your soul name you'll need to ascend the world tree, or whatever imagery you've designed for accessing the upper realms. Speak your request to the powers, then listen. Slowly, the music of the spheres will hush to a whisper, and in that whisper you'll hear your name.

Don't expect this to sound like any other name you've ever heard. The eternal soul isn't limited by language as are we. While some people get a very recognizable name, others hear an odd mingling of vocalizations, something constructed of all vowels or consonants, or a name that's formed from notes of music.

Whatever you hear, pay close attention and repeat it to yourself so you never forget it. Carry this knowledge safely back in your heart, using it on the earth-plane with all due discretion. While you might choose to share your soul name with a life mate as a sign of trust, this isn't a designation meant for common public knowledge.

Name Empowerment
Alternatively, you can undertake a shamanic quest to seek out a name that energizes a new spiritual path, empowers and integrates a life-changing incident, or a name that will help manifest a long-term ambition. While you can certainly ascend the world tree to learn this new name, I personally suggest starting this journey at the entry to the middle realm.

The middle realm represents the invisible flow and spiritual current of everyday reality. This exists around us all the time, just beneath the surface of things, even though we're rarely consciously aware of it. Since this flow often inspires the desire for a new name through circumstance and experience, beginning at the source makes sense.

Where you go *after* entering the middle realm to find that name will depend on Spirit's leading. You may stay on that level, and find your name carved into a tree, spelled out by a gathering of stones, or as part of a cloud formation. Or, you might travel elsewhere. In either case, once discovered, this name can be freely shared with others. In fact, the more you speak this name, the more its vibrations help finish the transformation process already begun in your heart.

Please note that this second type of name quest most often yields a temporary name. This name remains in use until your spiritual path shifts again, until life's circumstances impact your soul, and/or until various landmarks in your life are achieved. At that point, it will be time to venture forth again and discover another name that represents the best of the person you have become, and the adept shaman you hope to be.

POWER ANIMALS, TOTEMS, GUARDIANS, AND GUIDES

By definition, a shaman is one who develops a strong, lifetime relationship with helpful spirits, including those of the animal kingdom. In his or her studies, a shaman learns to talk to and understand animals and animal spirits in a fashion that we've all but written off as impossible in the modern world. Why? Because it is part of a shaman's role and responsibility to maintain that delicate balance between spiritual animals, their earthly representatives, and people, in all environments.

The shaman's relationship with the animal kingdom here and on the astral plane has many benefits. Initially it creates a greater affinity with and appreciation for nature, its symbolism, and powers. The essence of a animal guide or totem is such that it encourages earth-centeredness. The power animal already exists in harmony with nature, and since this spiritual presence isn't limited to a natural location, the power animal brings a bit of the Mother with it in all encounters.

Second, once a person finds a personal power animal(s) (or the animal finds him or her), he or she has the ability to call on that spirit to act as a guide or helpmate in other world journeys. A shaman may ask his or her power animal to accompany, carry, or precede himself or herself to a specific astral location. In some cases, the animal spirit may also choose to find a spirit or retrieve elusive information for the shaman's benefit while traveling the astral realms.

Note that in both the aforementioned situations the shaman voices a request to his or her animal companion, and not a command. Power animals, guides, and guardians are never subjugated by the shaman's will. When an animal is tamed or forced into service it often loses many of its natural abilities, because "nature" is no longer a part of the equation. For a spirit animal or its earthly representatives to maintain their distinction and potency, the shaman's relationship with them must always remain one of mutual respect and honor. Otherwise, the shaman risks losing or irreparably damaging that rapport.

Third, a power animal affords access to that totem's characteristics, attributes, lessons, and powers. For example, when a shaman needs strength he or she might call on the most powerful of his or her spiritual animal companions for aid or insight. Alternatively, a shaman may seek out an animal spirit other than his or her personal ones because that creature's inherent powers are more suited to a specific situation.

To accomplish this the shaman undertakes a middle world journey where he or she, or his or her power animal, bears a request to another specific totemic image. This request is sometimes accompanied by an offer of service in return for aid. This offer symbolically repays that spirit, whether or not the tribute is accepted. The gesture also represents the shaman's understanding of mutuality: that he or she must be willing to give to receive, to serve to be served.

Fourth, animal spirits offer safety, education, and reconnection. Some power animals are purely protective, and stand at the ready when danger threatens. Others come into our lives for a short period to provide us with the ordeals, trials, insights, or examples necessary for personal growth and accomplishment. Still others reconnect and reestablish personal power. When you walk with your totem, your ability to withstand dis-ease in all its forms improves; your ability to see, know, and manifest also improves.

Discovering Your Power Animals

There are several ways to discover your personal power animal(s). One is by using the Medicine Cards devised by Jamie Sams. This deck is an excellent introduction to many of the traditional power animals of shamanic cultures. The only drawback here is that the entire world is filled with creatures (not to mention plants and stones) other than those featured in the deck. Any of these other animals, plants, or stones *could* be your totem, guide, or familiar spirit. So, if you use this system, bear this limitation in mind.

Another way to uncover your power animal is by preparing yourself for dream work wherein you invite your animal guides to meet you in the dream plane (see Chapter 6). This approach can take days or weeks to result in a successful, confirmed dream meeting, but it's more comfortable for people who haven't really mastered shamanic journeying yet. It's also useful for those who find it difficult to release their expectations. No matter what you *think* your power animals are, the universe is likely to surprise you! While you sleep, you're naturally more open and less predisposed.

The third approach is the most traditional, that of undertaking a journey specifically for this purpose. To prepare for this journey, begin with a short period of fasting to clear your body and senses. For those who cannot fast, I recommend drinking plenty of water to clear out your system. Also spend some time in prayer and meditation in the days beforehand, expressing your desire to the Sacred.

When you're physically and spiritually prepared, create a sacred space, using a rattle at the four corners to announce your intention. Settle into whatever posture you prefer, and begin to meditate.

Return to your entryway to the middle realm. Pass through, get comfortable on the other side, and begin praying intently.

Voice your request to the spirits around you, then listen and watch patiently. Be aware that nothing might happen the first time you try this, or even the fifth time. Sometimes the spirit world tests our resolve and sincerity, so be diligent and keep trying.

When an animal finally approaches, ask if it is your guardian, guide, or power animal. The creature will acknowledge or revoke your query by physical movements such as a nod or turning away. No matter what the result, know that you have nothing to fear from this apparition. It has come freely, and if the animal doesn't feel an immediate empathy it will leave as quietly as it came.

By the way, you might be startled by what appears, and even question its validity. If you feel dismayed or uncertain, remember that your spirit is traveling the realm of infinite possibilities, so open yourself up. Even mythological beasts and insects can be personal power "animals." Don't automatically discount such visions. If you don't understand why a specific creature has come to you, ask it. You're going to have to learn to communicate with it at some point, so you might as well start off right.

Deepening the Connection
Just as with relationships among humans, the relationship between you and your power animal takes time and trust to develop fully. Each time you work with one you'll discover new dimensions to that creature's powers and personality. These dimensions ultimately reveal what role each power animal is best suited for, be it as an advisor, guide, guardian, or a spiritual friend and ally.

To improve the depth of your relationship with your power animals there are several things you can do regularly to help:

- Start learning as much as you can about the spirit animal's earthly representatives. The characteristics they exhibit are simply augmented in the astral landscape.

- Support and honor the totem's earthly representatives. Volunteer a few hours a week at a zoo, or make a donation to a reputable organization that protects that creature.

- Put paintings, drawings, or statues of the animal in various locations around the home. If you have a personal or family altar, leave one image there too. An alternative to this is wearing jewelry or carrying carvings that depict the animal.

- Whenever you greet the Sacred during your daily routine, also greet your animal.

- Invite your power animal to join you in any activities that you personally enjoy. This is akin to inviting a good friend for a hike, a trip to the museum, or to take a peek at your new craft project.

- Remember that the spirit realm and daily reality are always in contact with one another. So when your power animal's earthly representatives begin showing up in your life (physically, as part of advertising, in music, on business cards, or wherever) pay close attention. This is the power animal's way of getting your attention when it feels neglected, or when it has an important message to share. If you don't bother to respond, it's kind of like slamming a spiritual door in your totem's face.

- Ritually dance the animal to become more aware of it and part of it. In Chapter 2, we discussed how shamans use imitation as a means of manifesting something. In this case, you will be outwardly expressing the relationship that's developing within between you and your power animal.

- Shapeshift (see the next section) into a similar form and travel with your power animal to gain perspective and understanding. Let the power animal lead this expedition; this exhibits trust.

As you can see, a power animal is not merely a spiritual pet. It is a partner, friend, and ally in your shamanic development. Treat it accordingly and the relationship will always be mutually beneficial.

SHAPESHIFTING

The public-at-large often associates shapeshifting with what they've seen in the movies about a werewolf's transformation. This is an incorrect corollary that needs to be amended in your own mind before you can undertake a shapeshifting exercise. For one thing, shapeshifting is a personally controlled transformation, not something subject to the whims of a curse. It is not painful or dire, and most people find that shapeshifting is a very satisfying, helpful ability to acquire.

Shapeshifting is an ancient, well-respected shamanic art that allows you to temporarily don the astral image of a thing or person you wish to better understand, kind of like stepping into his or her shoes for a moment. This new set of shoes transforms the perceptions, feelings, and the comprehension of the practitioner, *not* the observer. Contrary to theatrical depictions, shapeshifting may or may not alter what others see or sense during the process.

Shapeshifting has no preconceived limits. You can embrace the image of an animal, a plant, a rock, a raindrop, a flame, a seed, or even a person with whom you wish to improve empathy. Some people reading this may find it hard to digest the idea that we can spiritually mirror something or someone else, but humans do this all the time without realizing it.

For example, when my husband was growing up he lived in an African-American neighborhood. He never even realized he was "white" until someone told him so, and even then he didn't believe him! Similarly, when you travel, don't you sometimes find yourself talking like the people of a region? These two examples illustrate a kind of environmental shapeshifting and mimicry that humans use as coping mechanisms. Now you'll be applying that highly adaptive ability in a spiritual construct.

TEN STEPS TO SUCCESSFUL SHAPESHIFTING

1   Decide who or what you want to become and *why*. Shapeshifting isn't something to do just for fun or for a nifty spiritual experience. It should have a definite purpose. For example, a shaman-healer may wish to become a specific herb to learn more about using that herb in his or her art. You might wish to shapeshift into the image of your power animal to build your relationship with that creature, and to better understand its abilities.

2   Study images of the object or person you wish to become. Do this over several days until you can see that image clearly in your mind's eye from any angle. It's very important for the portrait to have three dimensions. A "flat" mental image will not provide the right thought form for successful shapeshifting.

3   Decide if you want to use a costume or mask to help with the transformation process. If so, prepare one and have it ready when you start your meditation. Don the costume or mask at the outset, symbolically accepting the energy that it represents.

4   Create a sacred space. Shapeshifting results in a very deep trance. You'll want extra spiritual safeguards firmly in place.

5   Combine whatever techniques work best for creating a trance state and entering the middle realm. You may want to add thematic sensual cues to this process. For example, if shapeshifting into a forest creature, you might play a tape or CD that features forest sounds, or burn a woodsy incense like pine.

6   Call your power animal(s) to protect and guide you through this exercise. If you plan on mirroring your power animal, having it present gives you a ready model of what you're becoming.

7   Shed your physical skin and leave it near the entryway to the middle realm. Visualize yourself as having a body of light. You do not have

to be limited by the physical here. You also have the capacity to move and shift this light-body. It's malleable, like water.

8 Remind yourself that, on some level, you are connected to, and part of, all things. All you're doing now is moving beyond the boundaries that normally separate one physicality from another.

9 Bring to mind the portrait you studied before this exercise. See it like an empty cup or mold into which you will now pour your light-energy. Do this slowly so you can adjust to the new skin and its sensations.

  Be aware that your original pattern, the matrix of your soul, has not changed…only the housing. By merging with this housing you come to know it from the inside out, which in turn inspires understanding and harmony.

10 Follow your instincts once the transformation is complete. Pay particular attention to how your perspectives and senses have changed. You'll want to make note of these feelings and experiences later.

At some point after the shift you will notice yourself getting weary, having trouble concentrating, and/or the astral landscape will begin to get fuzzy or faded. This means you've accomplished all that you can, and that it's time to return and reclaim your natural matrix. Just as you poured yourself into the present shape, flow out of it, and put your skin back on. This will feel a bit like changing your clothes from head to toe. As before, do this slowly. Rushing the process results in disorientation, dizziness, headaches, and other unpleasant side effects.

Finally, ground yourself from the trance and make notes of your experience. Pay particular attention to what parts of the process seemed to help versus those that had no impact. You can use this information in preparing for future shapeshifting attempts, specifically in designing the right combination of techniques and sensory cues for a successful effort.

COMMUNICATING WITH ELEMENTALS

*Better remember how to put everything back
how we found it!*

—Barbara Kingsolver

Animistic belief systems regard everything in nature as having an empowering spirit, from a grain of sand to raindrops and the wind. Remnants of animistic thought still reveal themselves in the way we describe the elements all the time. How often do you hear people speak of an "angry wind," for example? For shamans, such characterizations have far more to them than metaphoric value. They represent the personality and power behind that wind—its elemental.

What Are Elementals?

Elementals are beings that exist inside the four basic spheres of creation (earth, air, fire, and water). They are creatures of raw drive and power, somewhat like an unbridled electrical current. This "current" gains a shape and characteristics from the element within which they flow. Beyond this, elementals also gain attributes and patterns from the specific sub-class of element to which they're attached. For example, the water elemental that abides in an ocean will be drastically different than one in a water spout. Likewise, an earth elemental attached to a flower looks quite different than one attached to a tree or the soil.

Why would ancient or modern shamans wish to establish a close rapport with these elemental beings? As an emissary between the worlds, the shaman knows that each elemental has a distinct voice that echoes across the middle realm. In traveling that realm, one should know how to hear those voices, understand them, and respond if necessary.

Moreover, the elementals exist in both the astral and the earth plane, being an intimate personification of nature and creation. This natural connection makes them an important ally for the shaman's work, especially for earth healing. Additionally, elemental powers can teach a shaman much about living and working with each part of his or her environment more effectively.

Element-ary Education and Communion

To begin your element-ary education, you'll want to introduce yourself to the powers in each quarter of the sacred space and spend time communing with each one. I suggest approaching each elemental separately for lessons, through a distinct ritual suited to its personality.

TEN STEPS FOR ELEMENTAL COMMUNION

1 Prepare some type of medium for your spirit guest so it will feel comfortable and welcome when it arrives. Suggestions include: soil, a plant, or a gathering of tiny seeds for earth; a cup of water, a running faucet, or a filled bathtub for water; a lit candle, burning brazier, or kindled fireplace for fire; an open window, a fan, tiny bells, or aromatics for air.

2 Prepare yourself. Fast if you wish, take a ritual bath, and spend as much time as possible immersing yourself in the base element of the creature you plan to call. Suggestions include: spending several hours gardening or walking in a natural setting for earth; dancing in the rain or swimming for water; sitting beneath the sun or in front of a heat source for fire; walking in the wind, focused breathing, or staying close to a fan for air. Remember: Like attracts like. By saturating your aura with an element's energy you'll increase the chances of establishing a good rapport with the corresponding elemental.

3 Create sacred space. This way if something goes wrong you have a controlled environment in which to handle it. The last thing you need is an angry or playful elemental wreaking havoc in your home.

4 Turn to the quarter in which the element you wish to contact abides and drum or rattle to announce your presence and intention.

5 Ask your animal to join you. It will often recognize an elemental presence before you do, and can also help you communicate with it more effectively.

6 Direct your breathing and focus for a middle realm journey. In some cases you may actually discover the elemental being waiting at your designated entryway!

7 Extend all your senses. If the elemental didn't meet you halfway, it will announce itself in a distinct way, such as rattling the seeds, making small ripples in the water, generating a gust of scented wind, or sparking a particularly bright and animated flame.

8 Ask the elemental what lessons you can learn from it, and what abilities you can hone through focusing on it. Be brief and sincere. Never command an elemental; this is considered very bad form. Being a good guest on this planet means respecting all the spirits who live here, and being appreciative when the spirits help you.

9 If you establish a good rapport with the elemental, ask it a name by which you can call it again. Establishing an ongoing relationship with the creature improves your capacity to work with its earthly counterparts. For example, my husband studied under a shaman whose rapport with fire elementals was so honed that he could reach into a blaze and carry out handfuls of tiny flames to light incense without harm!

10 Release the elemental back to its abode with gratitude. Nature has a distinct order, and a shaman always puts things back properly when a task is finished.

As with all other forms of trance work, make notes of your experiences as soon as you feel able. The fresher your recollections, the more serviceable the information will be in considering future attempts.

VISION QUEST

No man begins to be until he has seen a vision.

—Ojibwa saying

Of all the activities along the shaman's path, the vision quest is perhaps the most intimate. In embarking on this quest, the shaman seeks to understand his or her life's purpose, and to begin comprehending his or her true medicine (see Chapter 5, "The Medicine Wheel"). This time spent on the vision quest also renews our bodies and minds, reconnects us with the entirety of the spirit world, and reclaims the sacredness of self.

A traditional vision quest often requires a natural location, fasting, sleep deprivation, and up to four days of prayer and meditation. These elements sever the shaman from worldly thoughts and things, and encourage his or her being *present* and *real*. Once that severance has been made, sacred space is established and the participant waits, prays, and observes in stillness for the Sacred or the world to reveal itself.

Since we no longer live around abundant quiet, private, natural locations, the urban shaman faces some very real difficulties in his or her vision quest. If possible, I really suggest waiting until you can go on a retreat for a few days with like-minded companions to attempt a vision quest. These people will know your plans, and should wait nearby to retrieve you at a pre-determined time and place. Why? Because vision quests are mentally, physically, and psychically taxing. You will need a little TLC afterward.

If a remote location isn't feasible, see if you can "hole up" at home for several days. Get yourself some ear plugs to quiet the outside noises, turn off the telephone, and put up a huge "Do not disturb" sign on all your doors. Tell a trusted friend what you're doing, and have them come to check on you after a set amount of time. Also ask all your other friends and relatives to respect your request for privacy on this occasion. If your quest is interrupted, you'll have to start again from scratch.

In choosing someone to monitor your vision quest you are entrusting them with a very special duty. This person will be the first individual you have contact with after the quest. He or she will need to be very sensitive to your experience, and the energies that experience has created within and without. Consequently, choose someone with a gentle voice and heart for this task.

BASIC PROCEDURE FOR UNDERTAKING A VISION QUEST

1 In the months preceding the quest, try to work through issues that in the past have impeded your ability to focus. Also begin considering who you will ask to be your monitor for the quest.

2 For the week preceding the quest or even longer, eat very healthy foods. Avoid alcohol and sugars. Drink plenty of water and fruit juice. Also consider abstinence of some kind, such as giving up sexual encounters or red meat. This acts as an offering, and also reminds you of the importance of your quest.

3 Rise at dawn the morning of the quest and take a ritual bath, or ready a sweat lodge. Use personally meaningful herbs in the water. Pray for purification and preparedness. Notify your monitor that the quest has begun, and let him or her know when he or she should retrieve you.

4 Take only absolute necessities with you for your quest. Prescribe to the minimalist attitude, knowing that *you* are the most important part of the quest, not ritual tools, nor worldly things. Some drinking water is a good idea, as is a blanket if you're outside where the temperature may change drastically. Put your chosen items in the center of the area where you plan to stay for the quest.

5 Create a sacred space and call your power animals to guide and guard you in this quest.

6 Facing east, sing your shaman's song. Let this transform as before, crying out for a vision. Move yourself into the trance state so that you can see all three entryways to the realms. Ask that the path wherein you need the most vision open itself. Follow the portal that welcomes you.

7 Observe your power animal. Ask it to lead you where you need to go. If it doesn't move, sit down where you are, wait, and pray.

8 Keep waiting patiently. Spirit moves in its own time and ways. Many people report that they don't receive a vision until the very end of the pre-designated period, if at all.

Almost universally, you can expect certain things to happen to you during your time of waiting. First you will have to work past mental clutter, like wondering if you set up everything properly. Next comes tackling the physical discomforts that result from fasting and meditative postures. Once the physical disturbances abate, the emotional ones begin. All types of feelings emerge: You'll laugh, you'll get angry, and you will cry. Let these feelings flow out freely. After mind, body, and heart have expressed themselves, consciousness will begin to shift, and spiritual awakening occurs.

9 When, at last, your companion comes to check on you, instruct him or her to approach slowly and carefully so you will have time to adjust to his or her presence. His or her arrival signals the end of the quest. It's time to return through the portal. Take this *very* slowly, and let your friend attend to your needs.

10 As soon as physically feasible, write about or tape record the experience. Also share the story with your companion. Talking about the quest solidifies your experience and improves its clarity.

Don't be discouraged if you don't experience a "vision" on the first attempt, or even the third. Some people who go on a vision quest return with dramatic accounts of imagery and encounters. Others experience nothing more than profound insights generated by the time alone. Both results have quantifiable value that shouldn't be underestimated; both teach you about your medicine by nurturing and unlocking the perceptions of your inner shaman.

the medicine wheel: the pattern of wholeness

All things within this Universe Wheel know of their
harmony with every other being.

—Hyemeyohsts Storm, Seven Arrows

The Medicine Wheel represents far more than a system of healing. It symbolizes the vital force of the universe, ever in motion. It represents the cycles and the natural order of things. It embodies balance, life energy, and the pathway to understanding. Each person's "medicine" is not simply how he or she heals. A person's medicine is his or her spiritual awakeness, knowledge, and the lessons life has provided him or her. By comprehending our personal wheel we learn how to take fate in hand, apply our wills and intention, and create the magic of wholeness.

What, then, constitutes a shamanic healing philosophy? It begins in understanding that health is a combination of factors unique to each individual's life experiences and circumstances. Each person's path to wholeness doesn't just begin with a sickness and end when he or she recovers. It takes place over a lifetime by reaching or surmounting various mental, physical, and spiritual plateaus along the way.

Second, wholeness depends greatly on the individual's ability to reconnect. The urban shaman realizes that the most common culprits that generate or support dis-ease are fear, hard-heartedness, bitterness, spiritual closure, and self-doubt. When we face fear, it generates courage. When we unlock our hearts and spirits, it generates love, trust, and connection. When we express our real self, it generates confidence and proactive living.

Courage, love, self-reliance, and spiritual connection all improve the body's natural healing functions by opening the necessary energy pathways. Each of these pathways (the chakras), appears like little energy wheels—a perfect microcosm of the great Medicine Wheel whose lessons we are about to study.

THE WHEEL'S DIRECTIONS

Every direction on the Medicine Wheel has its own inherent powers and correspondences. These powers and correspondences differ from contemporary metaphysical practices, and often change slightly depending on the shamanic culture I reviewed. So bear in mind that the correspondences here represent a broad generalization to which you should add your own insights.

Studying the Medicine Wheel's correspondences is important for the urban shaman. Each point on the Wheel is like a miniature classroom for your body, mind, and spirit. Through quiet meditation, you'll begin to discern the deeper meanings behind the Wheel's representations, and the applications for them. Each glimmer of understanding is one giant step toward improved self-knowledge, integrated shamanic ideals, and (of course) augmented shaman-healer abilities.

North is the element of air and the region that holds the mind. This is the place of knowing, of clearing away what is not real and seeing what is. In terms of healing, north represents wellness that comes through wisdom and inner harmony, or that which comes through animals in symbolic or literal forms. Some medicines, for example, are extracted from animals, and other types of shamanic healing rely on a person's power animal for aid. This direction is aligned with the color white, the season of winter, the stars, and animals like the buffalo and horse, who move powerfully through their environment.

Shamanic east is the place of seeing. Here, dawn's fire illuminates one's spirit and releases our inner potential. For healing, the east offers an awareness of each person's power and path. This is also where we connect with the god aspect, recapture hope, stimulate inspired thinking, and learn to heal through joyful living. East is allied with the color yellow, the season of spring, the sun, creative inspiration, and animals like the eagle, who offer refreshed perspectives.

South is an intimate region close to the heart. Here we find the element of water that expresses our emotions honestly. The healing power of this quarter is trust, learning how to overcome our fears, and banishing negativity. Healing may also be found here in the gifts that come from nature (e.g., herbs). This direction is aligned with the color red, the moon, the season of summer, and animals like the mouse who symbolize the need for quiet and periodic aloneness.

The west is the place of looking within yourself and seeing what's *really* there. Within the earth's embrace, you will discover your inner priest or priestess, rediscover and reconnect with the mother goddess, become more accepting of change, and begin understanding the mysteries of life's cycles. In terms of healing, this quarter deals with the physical self, with taking care of our soul's temple, especially in maintaining proper mineral levels. (Note: This can be considered figuratively for healing amulets that are made from minerals.) This region also reconnects us with our tribes for stability, support, and well-being. The west is aligned with the color of black, the earth, the season of fall, and animals like bears (who hibernate in the earth's womb for a figurative rebirth each spring).

DIRECTION	PHYSICAL/MENTAL	MEDICINE POWERS
North	Brain; Knowledge	Harmony within Animal medicine Realness
East	Eyes; Insight	Potential within Faith medicine Perspective
South	Heart; Emotions	Truth within Nature medicine Serenity
West	Body; Structure	Stability within Mineral medicine Recognition
N-S Axis	Heart-Mind; Action	Attentiveness within Mindful living
E-W Axis	Body-Spirit; Power	Magic within Connected living

Between the north and south lies the axis that represents the heart-mind connection. This axis stresses the need to be mindful of the way emotions affect the way we think and act. Between east and west we discover the body-spirit connection. Here we're reminded that spirituality cannot be separated from the physical, or our magic—our medicine—dies.

The convergence of the two axis lines, wrapped within the Wheel's protective circle, shows that the Medicine Wheel is very holistic. It illustrates that every facet of the human being is important and worthy of our attention and care.

THE SHAMAN-HEALER

It is better to prevent than to cure.

—Peruvian proverb

Ancient people felt that sickness originated with an angered god, with improper actions that insulted a nature spirit, or from breaking taboos. In effect, sickness resulted directly from deceptive, inattentive, or unconnected living. As the caretaker of the tribe's spiritual and physical well-being, it fell upon the shaman to try and remedy this situation by mediating with spiritual forces on a person's behalf.

To accomplish this, the shaman often interviewed a patient first, asking about recent dreams and other significant events in his or her life. If the shaman decided that his or her medicine could help the afflicted, he or she fasted, prayed, danced, chanted, and entered a trance state. Then the shaman traveled to the astral realm seeking guidance and insight.

How long this whole procedure took depended on the severity of the problem, but eventually a cure was attained and communicated to the patient. This "cure" frequently took the form of offerings and actions that would appease the offended spirit and correct the patient's inappropriate living patterns. Without such correction, surely the sickness or another malady would return even worse than before. Alternatively, the patient might be instructed to wear an amulet and to follow a prescribed diet.

Modernly, urban shamans acknowledge the importance of the spirit world in healing, but know that this is only one part of achieving wholeness. Physical, psychological, and environmental issues all impact a person's well-being. Modern medicine also plays a role these days, and should be honored for its value. The hands of a sensitive physician can bear healing energy from Spirit too, along with his or her knowledgeable talents!

The difficulty for modern shaman-healers is twofold. First, we are all too often unaware of any problem until it evidences itself. It is hard to "prevent" dis-ease unless we're acting as ongoing spiritual counselors, guides, and teachers for individuals or a tribe, which isn't a responsibility to be undertaken lightly.

The second factor is deciding what magical or spiritual treatment will work best, considering the circumstances and whatever protocol modern medicine has prescribed. This determination depends heavily on the problem and the shaman's aptitude with various metaphysical healing techniques. Most shamans defer to the method they know best unless Spirit guides them otherwise. Even more importantly, this decision relies on a shaman being aware of his or her personal medicine and how to apply it effectively in a variety of situations.

Your Animal Medicine

Since you have undertaken the urban shamanic path, it is now time to discover your own medicine and how to use it effectively. The first step in this process is calling on your power animal for guidance and insight. Power animals often bear messages about personal medicine through their characteristics and associated symbolism. Some actually appear at times in our lives when we need that creature's specific healing energies.

Begin meditating and ask your spirit animal to join you. If you're doing this in a ritual setting, I suggest sitting in the northern quarter, the region that stresses animal medicine. When you feel that presence, communicate your desire to that creature, and then watch, listen, and learn. You may have to repeat this process many times before uncovering all the healing powers in any one totem, so be patient and internalize whatever lessons the spirit animal provides as it comes.

The following is a brief list that familiarizes you with some of the different healing powers that spirit animals confer. As you read, remember that your personal medicine need not be limited to a power animal's sphere, but it certainly will be augmented by it.

THE HEALING POWERS OF ANIMAL HELPERS

Bear	Heals through empathy and nurturing
Buffalo	Heals through prayer and forgiveness
Crow	Heals through shapeshifting or by applying universal law
Deer	Heals through emotional support and sensitivity
Dog	Heals with service and giving
Dolphin	Heals through breath and restores the life force
Eagle	Heals the spirit
Elk	Heals physical vitality and endurance
Fox	Heals by encouraging adaptation and resolution
Hawk	Heals communications skills and inaccurate perceptions
Horse	Heals memory and encourages balance
Lion	Heals by his or her life's example
Otter	Heals by teaching playfulness and renewing curiosity
Owl	Heals with insightful truths
Porcupine	Heals faith and trust
Rabbit	Heals fear
Raven	Heals using magical methods
Skunk	Heals through humor and reclaimed self-confidence
Snake	Heals by motivating active, participatory change
Spider	Heals the lines of a person's fate by offering alternatives and sound advice

Squirrel	Heals disempowered people, or those lacking energy
Swan	Heals intuitive senses
Turtle	Heals by counseling retreat, grounding, and protection
Whale	Heals through sounds (such as chanting or songs)
Wolf	Heals psychically, and through tribal reconnection

To illustrate: Those people with an eagle totem often have a strong affinity for channeling energy from the Great Spirit, and/or restoring other people after bouts of spiritual distress. Individuals with hawk totems tend to be catalysts for remedying a person's modes and methods of communication. In this manner, your power animal becomes an intimate part of your medicine. You can also call on other totemic images for help in different areas as needed.

Personality and Experiential Medicine

A healer's power is not secondary to his or her power animal's attributes. The healer works in tandem with this creature's abilities. This means that each individual's personality and life experiences change his or her medicine quite a bit. It also means that dramatic life changes can alter or accentuate that medicine.

As an illustration, I have always been a mothering type in my interactions with people. This personality provides a substructure suited to nurturing, teaching, and motivating medicine. In my early 20s I began studying and practicing herbal arts, which slowly blended itself into my medicine. Then, when I was in my late 20s, a severe accident heightened my psychic senses. This gave my medicine even more new dimensions: working with auras, psychometry, and spiritual empathy. Putting these various dimensions together, I can potentially sustain, reinforce, balance, or interpret energy patterns and imprints, depending on the problem at hand. On a more pragmatic level, I can also make an herbal tea, cream, oil, etc., for the physical condition being manifested.

Once you understand your animal's healing characteristics, it is time to think about how they blend with and augment your own natural abilities. In my case, I have an owl totem who brings the power of loving truth into counseling sessions. I also have a fox spirit who helps me teach people how to camouflage their personal energy and sacred spaces, which protects them against psychic attack. You will discover your power animals will help you similarly whenever you open the doorway for that assistance. Remember: A power animal is rarely intrusive unless something really important is at stake. So take a moment before practicing any healing art to ask the appropriate creature to join you.

HERBALISM

> *He that would know the reason of the operation*
> *of herbs must look up as high as the stars.*
>
> —Nicholas Culpeper

Around the world shamans have depended on nature's apothecary for assistance in healing arts. The botanical preparations that were used varied according to regional availability, but the concept behind them was always the same. Shamans trusted the Mother to help with the human quest for physical, emotional, and spiritual wholeness.

Today, many of the ancient formulas that were once considered a product of superstition have proven themselves effective in the hands of science. Better still, we have discovered that natural remedies don't exhibit the side effects that synthetic ones often do. In our effort to mimic nature, we overlooked the old axiom of "If it's not broke, don't fix it!" Many urban shamans, therefore, are starting to return to nature's storehouse, looking for organic wellness assistants: herbs that maintain or restore health.

Before sharing some of the common herbs that shamans have used for healing, I must issue caution. Herbalism is an exacting art, as illustrated by the herbalist's axiom that says, "If one can cure, two can kill." Cleanliness, measuring, timing, an intimate knowledge of plant spirits, and an awareness of the patient all affect the shaman's ability to heal. Therefore, I don't recommend jumping into herbalism with both feet. Start slowly by learning one preparation at a time and mastering it.

If you want to become more adept after trying the simple preparations, then I recommend diligent self-study. Compare ancient and modern texts that examine herbal arts spiritually and scientifically. Additionally, consider training with an accredited herbalist, especially one who integrates the spiritual dimension of plants into his or her work. In many states one must acquire a license to practice herbalism professionally.

The Herb Kit
There are literally thousands of plants that shamans used in healing around the world. I have limited this book's exploration to spices, fruits, vegetables, trees, or other common plants from early Native American tradition. A review of native herbals reveals over 400 botanical remedies. Of those, the following list reflects the items that are fairly available in and around your home, garden, lawn, or on supermarket shelves. This list is very abbreviated, so I heartily suggest adding information you discover from different shamanic traditions, and from herbalists whose work and writings you find helpful.

You will also notice that I have not gone into the spiritual healing applications for these herbs. Much of that information must be discovered by a shaman and his or her power animals through trance work. Here the shaman communicates with plant spirits directly (see the section on "Trance Healing" later in this chapter) to discern how best to use the plant's spiritual energies.

SHAMANIC HERBS AND APPLICATIONS

Alfalfa sprouts	Decrease acid. Use in salad. Decrease swollen glands. Drink as a tea.

Aloe	Burns. Apply the gel directly.
Aspen bark	Flu symptoms. Drink as a tea.
Asparagus root	Pain relief. Chew raw.
Beans	Itching. Mash into a poultice.
Beech leaf	Sore gums. Chew.
Birch leaf	Burn or bruise. Steep in warm water and apply the leaf to the skin.
Blackeyed Susan	Sores. Prepare a compress from the root.
Bran	Fever. Prepare a poultice with vinegar.
Cabbage leaf	Bruises and joint discomfort. Apply as poultice.
Catnip	Colic, indigestion. Drink as a tea.
Celery seed	Purification, insomnia. Drink as a tea.
Chicory leaf	Dandruff. Eat in salad.
Cornmeal	Bruises, swelling. Apply as a poultice.
Corn silk	High blood pressure. Drink as a tea.
Dandelion leaf	Skin conditions, blood cleanser. Eat fresh in salads.
Juniper twig	Acne. Pound into compress.
Mint	Headache, nervousness. Drink as a tea.
Nettle leaf	Cold symptoms, urinary disorders. Eat in salad or drink as a tea.
Oak bark	Pain relief. Pound into compress.
Oats	Laxative. Roast and eat two teaspoons for one to three days.
Onion	Infection. Bake into a poultice.

Onion juice	Insect bites. Apply directly.
Parsley	Itching relief. Make into compress.
Pine inner bark	Boils, acne, burns. Boil; apply as a pasty salve.
Pine nuts	Vitamin deficiency. Eat in salads or stir-fry to retain the most benefit.
Poplar bark	Fever. Drink in a tea.
Pumpkin	Burns. Mash the fruit into a poultice.
Raspberry leaf	Women's complaints. Drink as a tea.
Sage	Flu symptoms. Drink as a tea.
Strawberry leaf	Anemia, fever. Drink as a tea.
Sunflower petals	Joint disorders. Boil for a wash.
Sunflower seeds	Chest congestion. Eat raw.
Thyme	Gum problems. Gargle tea.
Walnut	Anemia. Eat raw or add to breads.
Watercress leaf	Weariness. Drink as a tea or add to soup.
Willow leaf	Toothache. Mash into poultice.
Willow bark	Pain relief. Make into a mild tea (two teaspoons bark to one pint water). Astringent. Steep in vinegar and dab on.

In applying the herbal information above, use the following formulas unless indicated otherwise.

COMPRESS: a cloth soaked with an infusion or tincture of an herb. An infusion has the same proportions as a tea, except you steep roots and bark for eight hours, leaves for two to three hours, and flowers for one hour. Seeds need only thirty minutes. Prepare a tincture by steeping one-half cup of herb to two and one-half cups alcohol (vodka is fine). Let this steep for one month, then strain and store in a cool area using an airtight container.

PASTE/PLASTER: Bruise the herb and mash it. Dampen with boiling water, then place between two pieces of gauze to apply. Some pastes can be applied directly so long as it doesn't irritate the skin.

POULTICE: Gather enough herb to cover the affected region, bruise the herb, and warm it with a little water on the stove. Cool to a temperature acceptable to the skin, then put directly on the affected area using a clean cloth to hold it in place for one hour. Replace as desired.

TEA: Steep one teaspoon dry herb or two teaspoons fresh herb in one cup of water for fifteen minutes.

WASH: Steep one ounce of herb in four pints water.

The Spiritual Dimension

Because herbalism is so popular these days, it's easy to whip up an herbal remedy and forget completely about the spiritual dimension. Since one of the goals of urban shamanism is honoring that dimension, try not to get caught in that trap. Healing isn't like fast food; you can't grab a handful of ingredients and expect them to satisfy everyone equally. By reintegrating the spiritual aspect, you attune each preparation to the person for whom it's being created, and thereby nurture the body-mind-soul connection.

How do you infuse an herbal product with spiritual energy? Recipes are very ritualistic by nature, so think of your preparation process as a mini-ritual. Return to Chapter 2 and look at all the elements in a ritual's blood, focusing on those easily added into your working space. Specifically, aromatics, prayers, your shaman's song, offerings, and symbolic movement are all very serviceable.

Burn an incense whose vibrations mirror your healing efforts (see Chapter 3, the section on "Home Aromatherapy"). Stand facing south (the area for plant medicine), say a prayer over each ingredient.

If you're picking the herb fresh, remember to thank the plant's spirit for its gift. Make an offering to the four winds, asking them to empower your mixture. Sing your shaman's song while you blend the herbs together, and stir counterclockwise so the sickness wanes. In the end you'll have a wonderful combination of practicality with vision that *feels* as good as it *heals*!

HEALING THROUGH THE ELEMENTS

> *The book of Nature is that which the physician*
> *must read; and to do so he must walk over the*
> *leaves.*
>
> —Paracelsus

It is no coincidence that we use the phrase "under the weather" to describe sickness. The elements (the weather) affect the way we feel every day. Ever notice that you sometimes experience an energy drain or a case of the blues after an overcast day, or find it more difficult to overcome a malady when the weather is stormy? In working with elemental healing you'll want to hone your awareness of these kinds of physical, emotional, and spiritual reactions to natural shifts in yourself.

The elemental healer also pays attention to how the earth's elemental patterns and powers affect others. Everything from magnetic fluxes and solar flares to a patient's location and altitude can dramatically influence wellness. By tracking a person's biorhythmic reactions during a particular natural cycle, the shaman can prescribe the right element to negate a problem. In the previous case of feeling drained during overcast weather, the prescription would likely take the form of advice: Get as much natural light, and sunlight in particular, as often as possible. This neatly banishes the gloomy clouds, has a scientifically validated healthful impact, and generally improves a person's attitude.

Beyond this kind of common sense, the elemental shaman uses earth, air, fire, and water as regular components in their healer's kit.

Fire

Fire purges sickness, energizes a person who is lacking in power and vitality, and/or rekindles the inner flames of someone suffering from impotence or a lack of love (including self-love). There are two safe ways to accomplish this. First, pass the person over a specially prepared fire to symbolically burn away the problem. A good option for urban shamans is jumping over a self-contained candle flame instead. In a ritual setting you may want to do this moving along the west-east axis of the Wheel to honor the fire element.

Second, rub a flammable object or cloth against the afflicted area, and then burn it to destroy the collected disease. Make sure you use a fire-safe container for this, and throw away the ashes afterward or bury them. This "puts away" the power of the sickness.

Water

This element is terrific for overachievers and disagreeable patients because it motivates restfulness. Water cleanses, soothes, and restores vital liquids to the body. For purification or calming effects, a person might be floated in water or passed through it akin to a baptism. Here we see the "death" and "resurrection" theme where the shaman attempts to fool sickly spirits into leaving the body. For those who don't live in close proximity to a flowing water source, a shower or sprinkler will suffice, but *not* a bath. Most shamanic practitioners agree that standing water is magically dead.

In a ritual construct, a person in need can be bathed from head to toe thrice to cleanse both body and the aura. For this, I suggest that the individual lie down on the north-south axis of the Wheel. The healer can then work from the south, washing the person in repeated waves, thereby honoring the water element's natural flowing movement.

For restoration and cleansing, one option is blessing a huge container of spring water and drinking several glasses a day until it is gone. Most people don't get enough water in their diets anyway, so this certainly won't hurt. Another option is tears, which have strong healing value as a physical manifestation of the water element. Try wiping tears on a cut or sore spot to anoint it with love.

Air

This element is best for emotional healing and fertility representing the renewed hope and abundance of spring. It is also excellent for lung conditions, symbolizing the vital breath. The simplest form of air healing is waiting until a day when the winds move from the north (air's resting place), and then going outside and taking in that air. When you can't get outside or the weather doesn't cooperate, try directing a hand-held or electrical fan for similar results.

The region where you gather fresh air can change its symbolism and applications. For example, go to a seashore to combine air energy with water (to clear away the stress that's causing emotional trauma), or go to a cave for air-earth energy (to clear away stress that causes physical trauma). Indoors, put a fan behind a bowl of water or on top of a large flat stone for similar effects, respectively.

Breathing on a patient is another shamanic approach that uses the air element. This represents opening a person's spirit for the work at hand, specifically by way of opening the aura to the shaman's talents. In modern times this idea has gained a very practical application: mouth-to-mouth resuscitation!

Earth

Earth is a tool for grounding, rooting, composting, and transmutation. Many ancient cultures partially buried a patient in a mock death so that death's spirit would pass them by. For our purposes this might equate to having a person sit on the earth so it can absorb negativity, and then turn the soil to turn the problem away.

Alternatively, an object might be touched to an afflicted area, and then buried in the dirt to similarly entomb the attached spirit. This concept works very effectively, especially if you have window boxes or potted plants. That way you take something negative and give it a positive place to transform. In round containers, put the object in the western quarter to honor the earth element.

Two other very practical shamanic earth cures incorporate clay and sand. Apply warm red clay to an infected area to draw out toxins. You can also spread warm green clay on sore muscles and joints for relief. Warm sand works likewise, and has the additional benefit of being useful in sand painting rituals.

Fire/Air

Pass the person through the smoke generated by a ritual fire from the east, moving north along the Wheel counterclockwise. The smoke cleanses his or her aura and carries away negative energy. The best alternative to this for urban dwellers is similarly using a ritually prepared smudge stick or incense blend, fanning it through the auric field.

Water/Earth

There are three easily adapted water-earth elemental methods you can try. First, mud packs are well-known for comfort and beautification. Second, gather the ashes from sacred fire and mingle them with fresh water. Sprinkle this on an afflicted area to banish sickness, moving around the Wheel from south to west counterclockwise. Note that this is an effective cleansing rite for a region, too.

Third, go to a lake or ocean and lie in sand near the water's edge so that the water laps up gently on you. Focus intently on letting your problems seep into the sand. When the tide goes out it will carry the sand and your problem away with it.

Water/Fire

Collect the sweat from an ailing person's brow on a small swatch of cloth. Burn the cloth in a ritually prepared fire. Or, wash the hands and feet of the afflicted thrice, pouring excess water on a ritual fire to extinguish spirit of disease. Finally, steam as a byproduct of fire and water not only eases congestion but is an excellent purifier for body and spirit. In a ritual setting, try to place the source of steam in the southeast quarter to honor both the water and fire elements.

Fire/Earth/Air/Water

One of the most beautiful artistic expressions of wellness is found in Navaho sand paintings, which incorporate all four elements into their construction. Traditional sand paintings can take up to nine days to complete. The process begins in a patient's home with a shaman, singers, and assistants who begin releasing sand (earth/fire) to the floor to create an image. This image summons powerful beings to help with the curing process.

Once the painting is ready, then the patient must be similarly prepared. He or she will be bathed (water), dried with cornmeal, marked with body paint, and adorned with turquoise (a healing, protective stone of earth). The shaman then sets a patient in the center of the portrait (amidst all elements) to illustrate the way to wholeness, and to symbolically bring the patient into unity with the spirits represented. At the end of the rite, the patient moves out of the sand so the shaman can ritually disperse it to the winds (air) or moving water. This also disperses any remnants of negative energy.

For urban shamans I see a couple of alternatives to a traditional sand painting rite. Both come to us through children's sand art sets, which allow you to decoratively fill a bottle with various colors of sand, or adhere it to paper. If done with a spiritual eye and a loving heart, the bottle could easily become a health amulet. In this case, choose the colors and color combinations that match the problem, such as mingling layers of blue (emotional healing) with yellow (creativity) for an artist experiencing blockage due to stress.

The paper works similarly, but I'd suggest that you pattern the sand on the paper to match the goal, along with its colors. Some traditional patterns include the images of Mother Earth and Father Sky, alone or together. Together they help heal respiratory or stomach ailments. Mother Earth assists with herbal and water cures, while Father Sky banishes depression and negativity. Other imagery follows:

SYMBOLIC IMAGERY

Bears	General healing energy and harmony
Black and yellow hues together	Masculine powers and guardians
Blue and white hues together	Feminine powers and guardians
Circles	New beginnings and hope
Mountains	Protective, nurturing energy
Paw prints (big animals)	Strength
Thunderbird	Energy; fire

To this list you can consider adding any personally significant symbols. Once completed, fold and carry the paper or display it where you'll see it frequently. Once the problem abates, burn or bury the paper with a grateful heart.

As you practice elemental healing, remember that shamans regularly added sensible first-aid techniques to these approaches. For example, if a person broke a leg, the shaman would first set and splint it, and *then* go on to mystical treatments. This is an excellent example to follow. Take care of the pressing physical issues first, so that valuable time isn't lost, and then go to Spirit to complete the healing process.

TRANCE HEALING

Through trance work a shaman psychically identifies and clears harmful influences that cause or support dis-ease. This process presumes, however, that a person *wants* help and has given permission for the shaman to do his or her work. Without this permission and trust, trance healings (or any other forms, for that matter) cannot begin. This rule is fundamentally important to every aspect of a shaman's duties. Good intentions aside, we cannot zealously sacrifice a person's free will or natural law in any of our practices.

Information Retrieval

One of the best applications for the trance state in healing is information retrieval. To determine a symptom's cause, the shaman travels the world tree, seeking spirits who will offer insight. If an offended spirit is found, the shaman asks about suitable reparation. On the other hand, a helping spirit discovered along the way can manifest the ailment as a visionary shape within the patient's body. Helping spirits sometimes provide information for curatives, too.

For determining the course of treatment, shamans can consult plant and stone spirits to know which herbals or amulets will help a person the most. The catalogued explanations of botanical and mineral cures hardly begin to describe the scope of nature's true medicine. Plant and stone spirits are allies in wholeness. Their unique language and unique qualities to affect different people in different ways is something only shamanic journeying reveals.

Specifically, during the trance state the plant spirits communicate when best to harvest a plant, what parts to use, how much to use, how to prepare it, when to administer treatment, and how long treatment should last. Stone spirits might recommend a specific mineral-laden diet, a combination of crystals for the patient to carry, sleeping in a ritually prepared stone circle for a healing dream, and the like.

The information retrieved from any one stone or plant spirit varies from patient to patient. This variance illustrates that each living thing vibrates on a very specific frequency, and the way that one frequency blends with another differs. Unlike humans who tend to follow fixed procedures, the cure revealed by a plant or stone spirit alters according to factors determined by the individual, the sickness, the timing, and the healer involved.

To try communing with these spirits yourself, meditate on the southwestern quarter of the Medicine Wheel (for nature and mineral medicine), and return to the middle realm of the world tree. Walk through this realm until you see a plant or stone that "speaks" to you. If you find you're having difficulty sensing which one wants to teach you, ask for the assistance of power animals like bees, spiders, and snakes. These totems have a close affinity with the plant and mineral world, and can lead you where you need to go.

Once you find a spirit who wishes to communicate, sit in front of that plant or stone and look at it with eyes of Spirit. Don't just view shape, colors, and textures. Look beyond the surface to see its magical, nonordinary aspects. Visit with the plant or stone as if it were a lifelong friend (which it can become in the years ahead).

When you're done, thank the spirit graciously and return. Make notes of your experience. After you've practiced this trance several times, and know the plant and stone spirits more intimately, then you can begin calling on them for aid in your work. By the way, plant and stone spirits aren't only good allies for healing. They can tell you much about magic and life as well.

Removing Intrusions

An intrusion is analogous to an infection, only on a spiritual level. For example, a shaman-healer might perceive evidence of a sore or torn muscle as a red protrusion in the auric energy field. This disrupts the body's overall balance and harmony, making it difficult for that condition to heal until the imbalance is likewise remedied. So initially, intrusion removal works within the auric field.

Going much deeper, however, intrusion removal must draw out a problem from the body, mind, and spirit, and not just from the aura expressing the problem. This threefold process often takes years of practice and training to master. Consequently, it is not a technique I recommend for anyone other than a serious practitioner with several years of experience in shamanic states of consciousness. Nonetheless, the method is so common in global shamanic tradition, that it warrants a brief description here.

To begin, the shaman calls his or her power animal for assistance, and then travels the lower realm (the foundation of the problem). Here he or she will often encounter a creature or other ugly imagery that somehow represents the intrusion. For example, a fanged serpent entwined around a person's foot might symbolize poison seeping into that body part. The shaman must overcome or banish that creature (and any others that subsequently appear) to continue the healing work.

Next, the shaman often begins a healing song and moves to the middle realm looking for other intrusions. These reveal themselves in the shaman's mind's eye as an irregularity in the body or aura, or again as a challenging creature to be overcome. Once discovered, the shaman moves to that region in the aura, sucks out the offensive energy, and quickly spits it out away from the patient. Haste is necessary so that the shaman runs no risks of accepting that energy into himself or herself. This process continues until no other irregularities can be found.

If the shaman perceives that a spiritual intrusion might also be a factor, he or she then moves to the upper realms and repeats the whole process once more. Otherwise, the ritual ends with a smudging and blessing, moving around the patient's body four times. This stresses the sacredness of the body, and invokes the powers of creation in maintaining that person's well-being.

Restoring Power

Shamans regard all illness as caused by some type of power loss. Various circumstances and people in our lives drain our power, akin to a psychic vampire. Specifically, anything that violates our free will or our sense of control, such as rape, terminal illness, or emotional abuse, depletes the vital force in varying degrees. This loss is characterized by statements from a person such as: "I feel lost"; "I'm disjointed"; "I'm tired all the time"; or "Why bother? My efforts won't matter."

When a shaman recognizes this condition, his or her duty is to retrieve and reconnect the missing life force so that an individual can begin recovering. The way a shaman accomplishes this depends on his or her astral landscape imagery. Generally, however, the shaman places a person on the east-west axis of the Medicine Wheel, and then moves into a trance state. From this perspective the shaman searches out the individual's energy thread (or whatever image he or she uses for visualizing energy) and follows that strand to wherever it splintered. At this point the shaman starts gathering the lost fibers together and carefully transports them back, returning the filaments to the patient's aura at the proper chakra (energy center).

The retrieval process can take several journeys to complete, and in some cases it can't be accomplished without a patient's direct participation. Since these strands represent segmented portions of self, some are too intimate for the shaman to handle directly. So, the shaman guides the individual into a trance. Here the patient might learn a personal power song that attracts and reintegrates the energy fibers. Or, he or she might find a power animal who helps gather those fibers. In either case, by going through this process the patient has taken an important step to reclaiming personal sanctity and his or her power.

RITUAL HEALING

All of the methods discussed in this chapter can, and often do, take place in a ritualistic setting. In fact, the ritualistic approach often manifests a greater amount of success. Why? Because ritual touches the innermost part of a person, and therefore facilitates the natural healing mechanisms. By using a ritual, a shaman provides a spiritually safe region in which to work healing, and also brings the Sacred back into a person's recovery processes.

In addition to the techniques and tools already reviewed, amulets and fetishes are two more that often appear as part of shamanic healing rites.

Amulets and Fetishes

Among the Pima and Papago Indians of the Sonoran Desert, the Sioux, and the Pueblos (just to name a few), the use of amulets and fetishes in healing rituals is quite common. The Pima shamans carve images of animals (fetishes) and lay them against the body of an afflicted person during a ritual to draw the spirit of sickness out. Specifically, a snake is used for stomach problems, a horned toad for rheumatism, and Gila monsters affect feverish babies. Comparably, a Sioux shaman might give a person a piece of turtle shell. The turtle spirit is said to ensure long life. Pueblo shamans applied bear claws and fur as similar amulets to prevent illness.

Out of respect for the earth, and by way of acknowledging previous abuses, urban shamans don't often use animal parts in healing rites. Nonetheless, there is nothing preventing us from using animal pictures or carvings instead, as Pima shamans do. Additionally, plant matter, stones, and many manmade objects such as keys (to unlock a problem or open the way for health) make serviceable healing amulets, too.

Here are some general rules for making and using healing amulets:

- Choose a token that has the appropriate symbolism, considering the person's condition. For example, one good token for someone suffering from chronic fatigue might be a stone carving of a lion, which personifies strength and endurance.

- Create a sacred space in which to prepare the amulet. This way, nothing other than the energies desired enter into the magical equation for wholeness.

- Ritually cleanse, bless, and charge the token for its function. Smudge the token, say prayers over it, and sing your shaman's healing song into the object. This breathes life and power into its matrix.

If you wish, also give the amulet an activating phrase at this juncture. An activating phrase is one word or a short sentence that "turns on" the amulet's power when most needed. This word or phrase is spoken three times to the object at the end of the charging process, and repeated once when you wish to mobilize the magic. One choice for the lion might be "roar," which is a show of power and dominance. To turn off the energy, just say the phrase again, and put the amulet away.

- Give the token to the individual at the end of a healing ritual as a parting gift to maintain or manifest wellness. Explain the significance of the toke if it's not obvious, and tell him or her the activating phrase, if applicable.

- Instruct the patient to carry the token regularly until the problem disappears.

- Ritually destroy the amulet when its function is completed. This totally negates the sickness's power (burning, burying, or tossing the item in water—if biodegradable—are all acceptable methods). This is also a sensible precaution that keeps another person from handling the amulet and accidentally picking up the negative energy.

Ancestral Healing

We are all born into a cultural unit. In shamanism, this cultural tribe and its history are very important to understanding and healing the individual. Unfortunately, modern history has been tainted by inaccuracies, which means that our perceived connections with culture and tradition are not always real. So how can the urban shaman uncover accurate information?

Based on the concept that genes carry memories from our Ancestors' experiences, ancestral healing begins with a trance state. To begin the process you'll want to journey to the upper realms, meet with the Ancestors, and listen to their lessons, which are also a part of you already. You just need to remember what's already deep within your heart. Each lesson you undertake will improve shamanic understanding, integration, growth, and ultimately your sense of wholeness and connectedness with the human culture.

From what I can tell, this can be a very time-consuming process, so be prepared. It may take months or even years to redevelop one's relationship with the ancestral powers. The longer a person has been steeped in the concrete jungle without touching the Sacred, the longer it takes. Even so, if you want to tap into your soul memory, the time is well worth it.

FORGIVENESS AND REPATTERNING

> *The practice of forgiveness is our most important contribution to healing the world.*
>
> —Marianne Williamson

Above and beyond physical-spiritual work, a healer-shaman often plays the part of a guide and counselor. He or she advises people on how to fight sickness actively, and live in a manner that maintains health once it is achieved. At least part of this advice takes the form of learning how to forgive and repattern.

Forgiveness reduces the stress that comes from feeling that our lives aren't the way they should be. It challenges us to accept whatever happens, and to act positively on it instead of wallowing in resentment, anger, and other negative emotions. Exactly where one aims the forgiveness depends on what's happening. If you hurt somewhere in your body, direct the forgiveness there. If you feel hurt by someone else or by circumstances, forgive that person or situation, and then direct forgiveness to your own heart. It won't cure everything, but I'm willing to bet you'll feel somewhat better afterward.

Repatterning is a little different. Shamanic repatterning shows us how to take a scenario in life and change the ending to manifest the outcome desired. In many ways this is a kind of sympathetic, imitative magic (see Chapter 2). For example, say you bump your elbow on a desk corner. Repeat the action several times, but change the ending so that your elbow misses on each repetition. This repatterns your memory of the incidence, and often results in your body changing to mirror that new memory. In this example the pain might abate more quickly, without any signs of bruising.

Physical repatterning is the most dramatic example I can provide. Much subtler forms of repatterning come through our thoughts and day-to-day actions. Someone with a tendency of self-denigration, for example, might practice positive repatterning through affirmations to change his or her self-image. This example shows how repatterning relies on the shamanic belief that life is what we *think* it to be. Ultimately the power to create change within and without begins with our thoughts.

Cradling work and story retelling are two other examples of shamanic techniques that use forgiveness and repatterning.

Cradling Work

This exercise is one that you may want to work into your regular spiritual routine. Three times a day, lie on a flat surface and hold yourself in an embrace. Close your eyes and lie in silence. During this time, think about any problems you've experienced that day, any aches and pains, and forgive them. If you made some mistakes that caused tension, forgive yourself and love yourself.

Next, consider ways that you can subtly repattern the negative occurrences of that day. See a positive outcome in your mind's eye. Hold the vision there until it's three-dimensional. Hold it as tightly as you're holding yourself so you can take it back into reality.

By the way, if you have a close friend who can cradle you during this exercise, you may want to try it together. Some people feel peculiar about holding themselves, so having a partner alleviates that awkwardness, and frees you to focus on the goal. A friend's embrace also generates a stronger field of love and trust within which to work.

Story Retelling

What cradling work does inside your mind, story retelling accomplishes with words. Story retelling starts with a known scenario, but repatterns the ending. Why alter a tale? Words have power; stories have power. As we hear them, and see the story with the eyes of imagination, we are drawn into the portrait. Once inside that world, the story becomes like the world tree that can transport us anywhere to forgive whatever needs forgiving, and bring back whatever we most need.

The basic story can be one from myths, a book you read, life's experience, or whatever, but it must be one whose theme matches your personal goal. In sharing the story with people, you recount it verse for verse, except for the last part where the magical transformation takes place. This is where you verbally create the energy and outcome desired in your own life. The more often you retell this tale with the changed ending, the more power it creates toward manifesting that goal.

☾

All the approaches to wellness discussed in this chapter can be augmented with two simple things: practicality and love. Practicality reminds us to eat well and rest. While our lives move at a pace that makes fast food easy, that doesn't mean that fast food is always healthy. So make time to serve the temple of your body nutritional food whenever possible, and perhaps take an herbal dietary supplement.

Love serves two functions. Self-love purges us of the negative feelings that often manifest themselves in stress-related illnesses. Love of others is the vehicle through which your shamanic healing arts flow, literally loving the world into wholeness one person at a time.

reaDINg the BONes: ways of seeing

Your sons and your daughters shall prophesy, your old man shall dream dreams, and your young men shall see visions.

—Joel 2:28

Seeing things differently and repatterning our thoughts and actions to mirror that vision improve well-being and many other aspects of life. But what happens when our vision is wanting, when no matter how hard we try, we can't see the positive or the possibilities? That's when the inner shaman offers alternative perspectives by both supernatural and natural means.

In the introduction, I mentioned that the word shaman means "one who knows." This designation developed because the ancient shamans knew how to read the signs in nature and those provided by other divinatory tools. This visionary gift also allowed the shaman access to other-world information and communications. He or she used these unique ways of seeing to foretell the future and offer advice on everyday matters including health, hunting, food gathering, the weather, fertility, when to hold specific rituals, and love, just to name a few.

This chapter discusses some of the shamanic approaches to div-

Eagle   Positive: restored health or a good break. Stay alert. Negative: Take care with your health or beware of an offer that seems too good to be true.

Frog   Positive: feeling rejuvenated in body, mind, and spirit; refreshed clarity; be thankful. Negative: a time of tears, but it will soon pass.

Hawk   Positive: good news; magical awareness. Negative: not seeing the truth, not living truthfully, or not taking responsibility.

Mouse   Positive: Organization and detail-mindedness will lead to success. Negative: beware of using your resources unwisely.

Otter   Positive: an opportunity for playfulness and leisure. Negative: lacking focus and scattering your attention on too many projects or hobbies.

Rabbit   Positive: abundance and fertility. Negative: Don't spend so much time thinking about tomorrow that you miss today.

Raven   Positive: manifesting magic. Negative: Karmic reprisal is coming to your doorstep.

Skunk   Positive: the ability to positively assert yourself. Negative: Egotistic attitudes are separating you from others and the Sacred.

Snake   Positive: recognizing the need to make a positive change in your life, and acting on it; initiate! Negative: Stubbornness leads to stagnation.

Squirrel   Positive: Preparation, planning, and integration afford success. Negative: Accumulations avail nothing; look for quality, not quantity.

Turtle   Positive: Creativity and solid foundations are yours. Negative: a blockage; the need to retreat and regroup.

Wolf   Positive: effectively making your way through a difficult situation. Negative: the need to develop a backbone and stand your ground.

In considering these meanings, look to any questions that have laid heavy on your heart recently, or pressing situations, and then adapt the interpretive value accordingly. Other factors to consider in your interpretation include:

- How did the creature move? Did it walk, run, limp? Walking indicates a calmness, running a more immediate need, and limping some type of impairment to progress.

- What was the creature's demeanor like? Friendly, pensive, fearful, angry? If angry, to whom or what was this ire directed? If toward you, you've somehow insulted your totem and need to make amends.

- What direction did the creature come from or go to? Generally, movements on your right-hand side (or left to right) are considered favorable. Alternatively, the direction of movement can indicate the direction in which a source of trouble or aid lies.

- What stance did the animal take? Standing, sitting, lying down? Standing is a position of readiness, while sitting can symbolize study or relaxation, and lying is submissive or restful.

To put this into an example, say you've had an argument in a relationship. Constantly seeing the image of a wolf with its hair up might indicate that (a) you are too angry to act right now without hurting someone or making things worse; (b) you need to act with all due resoluteness, bearing your teeth if need be to get a point across; or, (c) the other person is too defensive right now for you to accomplish anything positive. Wait a while and let this situation calm down.

Which interpretation is correct? Well, what else was the wolf doing? Was it running? Standing over a prey? These stances can conceivably relate to actions (b) and (a) respectively. So gather as much information as possible and add your own insights for the best possible results.

By Air, Water, Fire, and Earth

Moving into signs that originate with elements, the air can predict a child's future, among other things. For example, a child born during a northerly wind will have a wealthy life after some difficulties. One born in a west wind will grow up to master a common skill such as farming. Roaring winds at any time speak of troubles ahead, while calm warm breezes are a positive sign for that day.

For water, pay attention to the next rainstorm in your area. If it's short-lived but heavy and quick, you'll have guests arriving soon. If a body of water murmurs as you walk by, listen closely. A bubbling sound also presages guests.

Think of a question when building a fire or lighting any fire source, and then watch the salamanders who live within the flame for a response. Dancing, bright flames mean "yes." A low, sluggish flame is a warning to proceed slowly and cautiously. A fire that won't light or that goes out is a very negative omen.

With earth, every flower and blade of grass holds a potential lesson or message. Flowers like the daisy turn to follow the sun, teaching us the value of growing toward the "light," for example. Flowers growing in pairs might portend a relationship, while a tree dying often symbolizes war or other catastrophes.

There are many other bits of lore on how to recognize the voice of the elements when they speak. If you'd like to explore shamanic omens and signs further, many examples can be found in collections of folklore and superstition, and in books like *Futuretelling* (1998, The Crossing Press). But you don't necessarily need a book to comprehend earth's harbingers. Your inner shaman already understands far more than you think. The more you practice shamanism and commune with the spirits of nature, the more you'll become aware of, and understand, their messages.

Go to the world tree, and spend time in the middle realms. Talk to the elemental spirits there and ask them to teach you their language. It takes time, and you usually have to master one element at a time, but the effort is worth it.

NATURAL DIVINATION TOOLS

In addition to carefully watching nature's signs, shamans frequently turned to the earth's abundant resources for tools through which they could gain answers to pressing questions. Instead of random findings as discussed earlier, these tools were carefully chosen out of earth's storehouse. Stones, shells, feathers, dirt—these and many other natural mediums were made into divinatory tools to improve the shaman's ability to see those things that lie just beyond normal awareness.

Findings

Beyond observing happenstance occurrences in nature and traveling the world tree, sometimes shamans went more directly to nature with a question. In this case, the question was posed, and then he or she then walked the earth searching out an answer. The first stone found along the way provided a symbolic response by its color and the patterns on its surface.

For example, if the shaman wondered about the outcome of a forthcoming war, and he or she found a red stone, this might indicate terrible bloodshed. A white stone, conversely, represented a peaceful outcome. Square patterns advised that the tribe should plan further before moving ahead; an X represented the need for teamwork; a triangle symbolized fears ruling actions; a diamond indicated safety; and a line advised that inner fortitude was the key to success.

These interpretive values can be used for nearly any question, along with meaningful additions of your own. For example, if you find a stone with a circular pattern (or maybe a slab of blacktop), it may symbolize cycles, the turning wheel, or the circle of your tribe(s). Seeing a hand in concrete could mean that you need a helping hand to stabilize a situation. Or, finding a pin might represent the need to tighten up any loose ends.

Geomancy

Among shamans of Africa and other parts of the world, divination by earth seemed sensible. It was, after all, the most fundamental representation of the Mother. While several different approaches to earth-centered divinations were evidenced in shamanic cultures, the easiest approach was to make a line of holes in the ground while concentrating on a question. Don't worry about how many holes you make, just stop when it feels right. Repeat this procedure a total of three more times, making sure to maintain your focus. If you find your mind wandering, or if you get interrupted or experience other distractions, the system won't work. Try again later.

Once all four lines are completed, count up the number of holes in each line. An odd number of holes becomes a single dot and an even number becomes two dots. Write this pattern down on paper, or transcribe it in the dirt nearby, then check the following chart for meaning.

The interpretive values from the odd-even method seem to change from culture to culture. So, what I'm providing is an insightful amalgam of those interpretive values as they relate to materials already presented in this book.

● ● ● ●	A call to action; initiate.
● ● ● ● ●	A fresh start or opportunity; live attentively.

●
● ● ● ● Insight developing; integrate.

● ●
● ● ● ● Balance and success; live joyfully.

●
● ● ● ● Vitality and authority; stay truthful.

● ●
● ● ● ● Improvements, especially financially; be thankful.

● ●
● ● ● ● Obstacles or bondage; pray for aid or courage.

● ● ●
● ● ● ● Loss; meditate to find inner strength.

●
● ● ● ● Setbacks and troubles; use silence to find peace.

● ●
● ● ● ● Love, harmony, good relationships; stay real.

● ●
● ● ● ● Conflict; stay thoughtful.

● ● ●
● ● ● ● Wait and be patient; live presently.

● ●
● ● ● ● Luck. Sing your power song!

● ● ●
● ● ● ● Emotions dominating reason; breathe!

● ● ●
● ● ● ● Happiness, peace, and fulfillment; recognize and appreciate.

● ● ● ●
● ● ● ● Our tribes; reconnect.

If you want to get a little more detail in your reading, repeat the four-line process once or twice more, and see what patterns result. This should clarify the interpretation. Also, if you're somewhere that digging in the dirt isn't possible, a cake pan filled with sand, flour, or sugar can substitute. Easier still, just toss a coin. Heads is one dot; tails is two.

Shell Castings

This method appears among the shamans of West Africa, but has variations in Oceanic cultures as well. Gather four seashells, each of which has two defined sides. Determine which side of the shell represents female powers (spirals or curves indicate this), and which represents male powers (straight lines or angles indicate this). If you can't figure out which side is which, paint the sides two different colors (like black and white) instead.

Next, bless and charge the shell set somehow. Leave it in moonlight for intuitive qualities, sing it your shaman's song, breathe into the shells to give their spirit life, or provide them with a power phrase. Also, pray over them so that Spirit can help you use them more effectively and sensitively.

Put the finished shells into a basket and think of a simple question. With your eyes closed, keep concentrating and begin gently tossing the shells in the basket. When you feel ready, stop and look at the outcome. Four male sides facing you represents a positive response. Four female sides means "no." Three male sides up portends security, while three female sides predicts precariousness. Two of each indicates smooth sailing and the opportunity for personal growth.

This system can be augmented by adding more shells painted in different colors. If you choose this approach, interpret the outcome according to (a) the colors showing and how many of each, or (b) the pattern created by the shells.

Stone Castings

The use of crystals as a visionary tool has strong advocates in shamanic traditions around the world. Each tradition is like a cousin; they bear some likenesses to the overall family of stone divination, but also exhibit some important differences. Australian shamans, for example, wear stones and crystals in their navels, ears, and on other parts of the body to improve inner vision. In Latin America, crystals figure into vision-seeking rituals, and among the Kwakiutl Indians the winter ceremony is dedicated in part to quartz crystals, which are said to provide the shaman with clear sight.

From this brief study, it's easy to see that crystals hold an important place in core shamanism. For the urban shaman, they represent an easy and inconspicuous way to improve psychic skills while neatly providing a tool through which spiritual wisdom flows. The approach to stone casting that I'm sharing here originates in Hawaii.

Begin with a set of eight tumbled stones: red jasper or other red stone; carnelian or other orange stone; citrine or other yellow stone; malachite or other green stone; sodalite or other blue stone; amethyst or other purple stone; quartz or other white stone; and obsidian or other black stone. Note that you can get some small water-tumbled stones and paint them appropriate colors if crystals are too costly or difficult to obtain.

Prepare a special housing to keep the stones protected when you're not using them, and find a natural-fiber cloth that you can use for a reading surface. Bless the set in any manner you wish, and sing into them your shaman's song. As always, let this song vary of its own accord so the visionary aspect comes out.

Once your set is assembled, there are several different ways to use it. If you only need a "yes" or "no" answer, take out your green, red, and white stones only. Place the white stone in the center of your casting cloth. Hold the other two stones and think of a well-defined binary question. Toss out the two stones. If the red stone lands closest to the white, it means "no."

The second way to use your set is for gaining insight into a specific situation or action. This time use the black stone as the center point of your casting cloth. Think about the circumstances at hand, or the action you're considering. Toss the remaining stones on the cloth. Read the three stones closest to the black stone (no matter where they land) as the keys to making things work as follows:

Reading Colored Stones

Blue	Be confident of your abilities; practice realness.
Green	Apply love to this situation; reconnect.
Orange	Keep your eyes on one goal; recognize.
Purple	Stay flexible and go with the flow; live presently.
Red	Apply personal energy but avoid stress; be thoughtful.
White	Stay awake and aware; live attentively.
Yellow	Don't give up; pray for courage and strength.

If you don't like the outcome of a reading (the universe doesn't always have good news), reverse the stones, or move them purposefully to different locations. This is a kind of repatterning that allows you to take fate into your own hands. No matter the divination method, always remember that *you*, not your divination tool, are the master of personal destiny.

THE LIVING DREAM

The World is as you dream it.

—Numi, a Shuar Shaman (Ecuador)

Through dreams, people can receive messages and instructions that make everyday living clearer and more successful. We might consider this a form of divination; the shaman, however, considers it a natural expression of his or her relationship with Spirit. Through dreams shamans learn when to hunt, worship, fight, or feast; when to act, be still, to stand his or her ground, or to gather with family and friends. Dreams are effectively the shaman's guidebook for life.

Dream Aids

For people like myself who have trouble remembering dreams, core shamanism offers a couple of aids. The first helpmate is pre-bed meditations, prayers, and chanting. By taking time for quiet thoughtfulness and prayer, we attune ourselves to spirit. The shaman's song then serenades us gently into a trance state, which makes receiving and remembering a significant dream more likely, not to mention a decent night's sleep!

The next helpmate is the ever-popular dream catcher (see crafting instructions in Chapter 9). For readers who have never seen one of these, it looks like a spider web inside a circle formed by twigs. Tiny crystals, feathers, and other power objects are attached to the web. The circle represents the Medicine Wheel. The web keeps out nightmares, catches good dreams, and then filters them down to the sleeper. Finally, the power objects augment the significance of this tool and attune it to the practitioner. For example, one of my animals is an owl, so my dream catcher includes a found owl feather in its construction. This feather welcomes that power animal into my dreams as a messenger or guide.

Dream Interpretations

Not all dreams have deep spiritual significance. In fact, most give us alternative views of a day's events or things weighing heavily on our minds. Even among the spiritually inspired dreams, some are pretty straightforward. For example, if a power animal appears in your dream, it probably wants to tell you something. So, ask it! This is your dreamscape, and you have the means to interact with it. Write down the animal's answer when you wake up and meditate on it later for more significance.

Other significant dreams contain a central symbol, object, or theme that reflects the dream's main message for you. The following list is an abbreviated dream dictionary showing some common associations for a dream's theme. In addition to these interpretive values, bear in mind your present situation, any worrisome matters, environmental influences, conversations, and other such things that can sway the contents of your dreams (see also *The Language of Dreams*, The Crossing Press, 1997).

DREAM KEY

Accident	Some type of warning; danger ahead; stay attentive.
Acorn	Potential, but also a warning not to be too rigid; learn the value of flexibility.
Air (wind)	Pay attention to your thoughts and recognize how they're affecting actions or communications.
Amulet	Trust too much in "things" instead of yourself and Spirit.
Animals	Varies by type, but this often indicates a type of fetish or medicine bundle you need to make.
Antelope	Take another tact with a pressing problem.
Ants	Usually a good sign of improved finances. Be patient and live presently.
Ashes	Some type of ending, but the aftermath will be positive. Integrate the lessons.
Autumn	An opportunity to reap the rewards from your hard labors. Give thanks.

Axe	Trouble; a path, person, or opportunity being cut off. Stay true to yourself.
Basket	Pay attention to what this contains so you know what to gather for yourself or a situation. Internalize.
Bat	Forthcoming crises; prepare.
Bath	Purify and cleanse yourself or the item shown.
Bear	The need for either (a) retreat, (b) to emerge from a time of retreat, or (c) to build courage.
Bees	Good work brings harmony and life's sweetness. Enjoy! Alternatively, unexpected good news
Bones	Foundations of a figurative or literal nature (note the condition of the bones for more insight); structure
Buffalo	A driving force; the need for fortitude; persevere. Alternatively, unexpected support for a special project
Butterfly	Renewal; transformation. Initiate!
Cat	Aware living; the ability to recoup in a difficult situation
Cave	The need to reconnect with the Mother spirit and get some much-needed silence
Charms	Dependence on objects over the self and the Sacred; look at the charm's shape for more insights.
Child	A promise of your tribe's continuance; hope
Clay	Stay flexible; you have the power to design your life and fate.
Comet	An awakening or message coming to you
Coyote	Being misled somehow, but you'll learn something valuable here.
Crow	Stay on the designated path and don't stray.

Crystals	Spiritual focus (the color often indicates in what areas your talents lie, like red for love, or yellow for communicating spiritual ideas)
Dancing	The pace of your life, and the level of your joyfulness; what type of dance do you see?
Deer	Stay aware and alert, but walk gently in this situation.
Desert	A call for a personal retreat. Live thoughtfully.
Dog	A friend or other close relationship. The dog's condition indicates more. Reconnect.
Drum	The voice of the Ancestors or Spirit is calling you.
Duck	A person whose motives you've questioned offers aid.
Eagle	Freedom and liberation; perspective
Earth	The grandmother spirit; the feminine powers of the universe
Earthquake	Spirit's wake-up call
Eating	Internalizing and integrating an idea, a skill, or some type of knowledge
Eyes	Your ways of seeing and perceiving. Look at the color of the eyes and their condition. For example, being blindfolded means you're missing something.
Farming	Plant and cultivate the seeds of character and spiritual talents you desire.
Feast	Abundance and a reason to give thanks
Feather	A communication from Spirit is coming soon; live prayerfully
Fire	Your emotions and passions; in what condition do you find the fire?
Fireplace	Emotional warmth and love. Is there a fire burning?

Fish	Success comes from applying your skills.
Fishing	A search. Live attentively to catch what you most desire.
Frog	Sickness; alternatively, a physical or spiritual cleansing.
Grain	Providence and continuance.
Grave	A spirit lurks nearby, wishing to be appeased by correct behavior.
Hawk	A trustworthy friend hovers close.
Herbs	Natural healing sources that you have available, but may not be using. Alternatively, a plant spirit speaking to you.
Historical Items/Places	Living in the past instead of presently. Alternatively, a past-life memory
Horse (or car)	The vehicle of your life; what condition is it in? How quickly or slowly is it moving?
Hummingbird	Staying balanced brings joy.
Incense	A cleansing; a prayer, or wish rising to Spirit's attention
Kitchen	Gather with those you love and preserve that unit. Alternatively, what kind of figurative foods have you been consuming lately?
Lava	The need to release your anger before it boils over
Lightning	A curse or severe warning from Spirit
Lion	Don't be overly ambitious.
Lizard	The keeper of dreamtime; you'll be getting more significant night visions.
Lynx	A secret will be revealed.
Masks	The ability to transform and repattern. What does the mask depict, and what happens to it?

Medicine Shield	Pay attention to your health; or, look to see which part of the shield is predominant to understand the shield's message.
Mirage	Living in an illusion. Begin practicing truthfulness and realness.
Mirror	What do you see here? Are you seeing yourself clearly? Work toward self-acceptance.
Moon	Changeability; the grandmother aspect of Spirit, especially when full.
Mountaintops	Power coming to you
Net	Something being captured or entrapped. What's in the net?
Owl	A message from Spirit or your own Higher Self to stay true to your ideals and taboos
Paint	An important personal transformation is coming; prepare yourself
Parrot	Someone who speaks half-truths.
People (a group)	Your tribe(s). See where you fit in and how you interact in this dream.
Pipe	A call for peace; a call to prayer
Pollen	You're running the risk of losing your way.
Rabbit	Fear, often of intimacy
Rat	Clean up your act.
Rattle	An announcement or introduction
Ritual	Honoring the Sacred; time to gather with like-minded people. What's the ritual for?

Rope	Our ties to people or situations. Recognize them and begin reconnecting.
Seashell	Messages, often of a spiritual nature
Sky	The grandfather spirit; the masculine force of the universe
Smoke	A message from your tribe, the Ancestors, or Spirit
Soil	Pay attention to physical needs and conditions.
Songs	Listen to the words—this may be a new power song for you. Alternatively, an infusion of a specific type of energy you need from Spirit
Spider	Untangling of a knotty relationship followed by financial improvements
Spring	Renewal, fertility, and hope. Something is changing for the better.
Stars	Your quest; the desire for truthfulness; wishes
Summer	Personal fulfillment, often of a social nature
Sun	Hope, blessing; the grandfather aspect of Spirit
Talking Stick	Communication; do you need to take this or hold it?
Tattoo	Your history and traditions, and an encouragement to maintain them
Teepee (or house)	Tend carefully the tribe of people who live here, even if it's a tribe of one.
Thunderbird	A messenger who bears truth, even if it's harsh
Tiger (or great cats)	Aggressive power
Tornado	Tumultuous times ahead; ground yourself.

Tree	The world tree; possibly a call to travel it for understanding or discovery
Turtle	Slow, steady progress is the key to success. How does it appear? If its head is in the shell, stop being a wallflower and start living.
Valley	A place of rest and relaxation; take a break and integrate what's happened recently.
Venomous Creatures	Something or someone is trying to poison your beliefs or outlooks. Don't let them.
Volcano (eruption)	A message from the Mother, and she's not happy with you. Are you living in reciprocity?
Walking	Movement or change that's motivated by personal choice(s)
Walking Stick	Careful movement; a magical focus.
Warrior	Dedication and determination; the willingness to fight the good fight
Water	Pay attention to spiritual matters and messages.
Whale	Spirit is guiding your present situation.
Wind	Your ways of thinking and communicating. Strong winds, for example, indicate a blustery personality that spouts off without a lot of thought.
Winter	A time of waiting when little change will be seen externally, but is happening within
Wolf	Don't trust a person or situation that seems too good to be true.

When such obvious key messages, symbols, and themes seem wanting, then Spirit becomes the vehicle for the shaman's understanding. Ask your spirit animal or guides for assistance. Ascend the world tree and explore until you find the insight you need to clarify the vision and learn how to apply it to your life.

Dream Repatterning

Dreams have a language all their own. This language reflects the mind's understanding of things in literal or symbolic form. While immersed in that form, we don't question its validity; it just *is*. This acceptance releases the human mind from concrete modes of thinking and perceiving, thereby allowing for some really creative innovations.

By altering the format of a dream, we can potentially change our understanding and awareness. We create a new, more positive pattern from which to work, live, and interpret Spirit's messages to us. Modernly, this is called lucid dreaming, where a person willfully changes the direction, landscape, and outcome of a dream with a specific goal in mind.

How does this fit into divination? Well, say you have a dream of the future, but it isn't what you hope. At the point where you see things going badly, use the skills you've honed in meditation and visualization, and transform the dream. Call to your animal spirit or other astral helpers for aid. Create the tools, words, scenery, or whatever else is necessary to turn the negative landscape into a positive one. That way, you're seeing the future in a good light, and can carry hope in your heart instead of fear. Believe me when I say that hope is a potent ally in transforming the course of our reality.

I should note at this point that this kind of repatterning works well with daydreams too. Daydreams are simply an adult imaginative release. The power of our imagination to change both today and tomorrow shouldn't be underestimated. If we can think it, we can be it, but we have to be willing to try first.

OTHER DIVINATION METHODS

Urban shamans continue to turn to Spirit for insights when personal vision, or that of someone in the tribe, is clouded or when pressing matters arise. There are a lot of methods you can choose from, not all of which have to originate in shamanism. The purpose of this section is simply to familiarize you with some other customary approaches so you can make an informed decision on the best divination system for you.

Crystal Scrying

Shamanic ways of seeing depend strongly on the belief in life's interrelatedness, and on a person's capacity to interpret messages from nature's various kingdoms, including the mineral kingdom. Australian shamans, for example, revere crystals and use them in divinatory rituals, believing them to be a gift from the Rainbow Snake, a life-giving deity. By going into a trance, and making himself or herself one with the spirit that abides there, the shaman receives visions that answer the question at hand.

Other similar practices are found in the Yucatan and among Native American tribes. In the Yucatan, any clear stone can become a vehicle for scrying, while the Apache shamans use special crystals to find stolen or lost property. The Cherokee also had divining crystals that they ritually fed with animal blood to retain the tool's power.

To try crystal gazing in your own practices, follow or adapt this procedure:

HOW TO PRACTICE CRYSTAL GAZING

1 Cleanse your stone in pure water or saltwater to make sure it is free of any unwanted energies.

2 For at least a week, carry the stone with you and sleep with it under your pillow. This acts like a letter of introduction to the stone spirit, and improves the stone's sympathy with your energy. Try, however, to keep it out of sunlight. Some shamanic traditions feel this light robs the stone spirit of its power.

3 Before using the crystal, feed its energy somehow. Some earth-friendly ways that shamans did this included rubbing the crystal with special herbs, passing it through incense, or dipping it in rum.

4   Place the crystal on a dark surface, preferably on a stand that allows full viewing of the stone.

5   Begin singing your divinatory song, or allow your shaman's song to adapt to this process. Breathe deeply and slowly, moving yourself into a receptive trance state.

6   Gaze toward the stone, but not directly at it. Let your vision blur a bit, watch, and wait for at least five minutes.

7   At some point shapes, colors, clouds, or pictures will start forming on the crystal's surface. Watch them as you might watch a movie, trying not to *make* them happen, just let them form and reform. Make a mental note of what you see.

8   When the stone goes blank, you've received all the information you can in this session. Change your breathing pattern back to normal, and make notes of your experience.

9   Afterward, whisper words of thanks to the stone spirit, then store the stone in a special place, such as a power pouch.

Note that a scrying stone can have other applications including healing, pendulum work, and inspiring dreams. For the latter, if you wish to ask the stone for personal advice, carry it in your pocket all day, then take it to bed. According to Yuman shamans, the stone spirit will then grant visionary dreams.

Drum Head Method

In Chapter 2, I explained the importance of drums in nearly all shamanic techniques and rituals. Divination is no exception. Besides helping the shaman reach an altered state of awareness wherein he or she can interpret divinatory systems accurately, the drum itself can also be a tool for fortunetelling.

These particular methods of divination appeared in Siberia and among Laplander shamans. In one version, a token like a ring or a piece of horn was laid on the drum head. A person would continually voice a question while the shaman struck the drum head. The movements and final resting spot of the token were then interpreted for an answer.

In another version colored bits of corn, variegated seeds, or different types of beans were placed on the drum's surface. The shaman then looked for patterns to form out of the medium from the drum's vibrations. To improve the interpretive values of this system, some shamans painted the drum head with symbolic indicators, such as those for the four elements. They then interpreted the reading according to how many tokens landed in various locations and any obvious imagery in the token's patterns. In this manner the drum head became a miniature Medicine Wheel upon which the fates patterned themselves in harmony with natural order.

If you own a drum, this system is fairly easy to duplicate. Even if you don't, a nice flat pan will suffice (although I don't recommend using aluminum; try iron).

DIVINATION THROUGH DRUMMING

1 Decide what types of tokens you wish to use for your efforts.

2 Determine the tokens' meanings depending on where they come to rest on the drum head and make notes of those meanings so you can use them regularly. Consider numeric symbolism, color representations, the meanings of the four quarters, and even each type of seed, bean, or whatever, for possible significance. While you don't have to integrate all these potential indicators, you should at least consider which ones will work best for you.

3 Decide if you want to mark your drum head with personally significant symbols. If so, how will these symbols change the interpretive values of your tokens or medium?

4 Put the drum on a flat surface that isn't easily moved, like the dining room table.

5 Place your strong hand in the center of the drum head and move it around the top three times, clockwise, while thinking of your question.

6 Put the tokens or medium in the center point of the drum.

7 Pray, chant, or sing your shaman's song until you feel your awareness shifting.

8 Begin tapping the drum head with your eyes closed. Continue until you feel Spirit's leading to stop.

9 Open your eyes and ponder any immediate impressions you get about the final resting places or patterns created.

10 Compare the resting places and patterns with your notes and then interpret the outcome by combining your notes with your first intuitive insights.

Last, but not least, remember to make notes of the reading and your experience during it for future reference.

Medicine Shield

This is an interesting use for your medicine shield that I stumbled across in my readings. Take your shield firmly in both hands and close your eyes. Think of a binary question (one that has two possible answers, like yes/no, wait/act, good/bad, etc.). When you've finished focusing your energy, roll the shield on its edge along the ground (obviously your shield needs to be round for this to work). If it lands face up the omen is a positive one.

Doing this regularly can be a bit rough on the shield, so you may want to construct one especially for this purpose (see Chapter 9, "Applied Urban Shamanism"). In this case I suggest using a round flat of lightweight wood or other sturdy material with well-sanded edges. On the surface of the shield paint symbols that, to you, represent insight and understanding (like an open eye or something similar).

Bless the shield and empower it with your shaman's divinatory song, then give it a roll!

To increase the potential interpretations here, quarter the shield and paint each quarter an elemental color. When the shield lands face up, the omen is still positive, but it is augmented by the color/quarter that's closest to you. Say, for example, you asked about your present relationship, and then rolled the shield. The red side (south) landed closest to you, facing upward. The interpretation here might be that the relationship is good as long as both partners stay honest and real.

Trance Divination

As the diplomat between this world and the astral reality, a shaman may undertake a trance journey to gain insights for another person or for himself or herself. For personal answers to simple questions, such a journey often begins and ends with a meeting between the shaman and his or her power animals. Here the question at hand is posed directly to the creature, who then answers somehow. Most commonly the animal will answer through one of three ways:

(a) Its movements. For example, if you asked whether or not it was wise to proceed along a specific course and the animal sits or lies down, that would mean, "No. Stay put."

(b) Taking the shaman to other levels of the astral reality where the landscape or experiences answer the question. Using the same question/response scenario, the shaman might be shown an astral river whose path has been cut off or altered in some way.

(c) Empathically. In this the shaman might simply "feel" that moving ahead is the wrong thing to do.

If you decide to try this yourself, don't ask overly complicated questions at first. It takes a while to hone your comprehension of the power animal's responses. Also, consider having a tape recorder handy so you can recite your experiences as they happen. This will provide you with a valuable record of insights that you can review any time.

In seeking answers for someone else, the shaman will often spend a significant amount of time with the inquirer, coming to understand him or her, defining the question, and acquainting himself or herself with the individual's energy. Without this personal touch, the astral landscape described will likely hold little meaning for the inquirer. Additionally, this time together helps the shaman transport a little of the inquirer's personal energy with them into the other realm, making the outcome more significant.

So, if you accept the responsibility of seeking out answers for someone else, begin by spending quality time with him or her. After you feel comfortable and completely informed, you can then move into a trance state. Once you travel to the world tree, call upon your power animals and guides once more. Tell them your mission. They will lead you where you need to go.

Don't try to make this landscape or its imagery conform to something *you* understand. Remember: This journey isn't for you, so the landscape and sensations will be ones to which the inquirer relates. Describe everything you see and experience as you go, having him or her tape record the journey or take notes. Keep this information very detailed. Even minute points can be important (bigger is not necessarily better in astral reality).

When you feel the journey is complete (your guides or power animals will often indicate this by bringing you back to the entryway to the world tree), return to normal awareness. Ground out a bit, and then talk about the imagery with the inquirer. It's not your job to explain it to him or her, or try and infer meanings, but you do need to be a good counselor at this point and listen. Listen to the person's questions and offer options for his or her consideration. Help the individual integrate the information from the journey to the best of your ability.

Also, instruct the inquirer to listen to the tape, or read the notes several times over the ensuing days and weeks. Each time the inquirer does so, he or she will find something new to ponder, or discover another insight into his or her situation. As the individual reviews the journey he or she may want to return to you with more questions. Shamanic imagery isn't easily understood by everyone, so try and make time for those questions, and answer them with a gentle voice. If you treat the inquirer in the same manner as you would wish for a reading, you'll never go wrong.

☾

Many other shamanic divination methods exist beyond those that I can easily discuss in this format. There are even more that can come from your own devising! Think about it. Somewhere along the way a sage or seer had to decide among nature's gifts for something that helped tap the superconscious. The actual item wasn't half as important as the process of self-reliance going on within.

Shamans both past and present knew that a tool is just a tool; you are the enabler—the one who breathes a magical vision into that implement. In truth, shamans need no stones or signs. Seeing things differently is a natural outcome of participatory, attentive living. So the only real tools you need for divination are faith, awareness, and *you*.

the papoose: children of the tribe

It takes two people to make a child,
but a tribe to raise one.

—old Hopi saying

In days gone by, a tribe could easily die out without an abundance of children to carry on its knowledge and traditions. Consequently, core shamanism sees children as having a very important role: They represent the hope of the future and the tribe's continuance. It is therefore the responsibility of shamans to help further the spiritual, intellectual, and cultural development of the tribe's children.

For the urban shaman, things are a little more difficult and different. We face a somewhat intolerant society that doesn't always accept or understand our beliefs and practices. We can't easily take the children in our lives on long retreats, or move them into kivas for education at the knees of the elders. In fact, much of our children's education is out of our hands altogether, taking place in the schools. Nonetheless, it falls on those walking a shamanic path to help our children's spirits to grow to fullness alongside their minds.

For the sake of simplicity, this chapter is written from the perspective of a parent to other parents. However, those of you reading this who don't have children, please familiarize yourself with the ideas here anyway. There are likely to be a few children around you (cousins, nieces or nephews, children of neighbors, and the like) who could benefit from simple shamanic insights and lessons. Sharing these doesn't equate to proselytizing; nature's lessons are not dogmatic, and the most important lessons of shamanism are those that children naturally understand: realness, joyfulness, and present living.

THE WAY THEY SHOULD GROW

Every major world religion teaches children in the ways of that belief system. Because of the neo-pagan belief that each person should find her or his own path to the Divine, many people in the metaphysical community are confused or uncertain about teaching children magic. This need not be so.

To my thinking, one of the greatest gifts we can give our youth is a belief in self, in Spirit, and in the wonders and potentials of the universe. Additionally, children are some of the wisest, most adept shamans I've ever met. Many exhibit a natural ability to understand the elementals, see spirits, communicate with animals, and weave their wills into spells without a second thought.

In order for any family's love and traditions to thrive, children should be taught to honor that unit and its beliefs. Building a respectfulness toward the Sacred, the earth, and others is something that will reach far beyond a child's religious system or family customs. It is an *honest* way of thinking and being that will benefit a person throughout his or her life, even if he or she grows up and takes a different path.

As the parent of three very curious children, I've found myself confronted with difficult spiritual and social issues. Among them has been how much magic to teach, when to teach it, and how to express it so that teachers, neighbors, relatives, and playmates don't get nervous. This isn't an easy call because you find yourself caught between being totally honest, and giving children only partial knowledge with flowery images to keep other people comfortable.

Only you know the tolerance level of the people around you and your region, so instruct children accordingly. Find generic, universal symbols around which to construct the core of your children's lessons. For example, "white light" is an excellent description for Spirit's presence and protective power. It's also a term that has been used so much in New Age vernacular as to be quite commonplace and nonthreatening. Calling god/dess the Great Spirit also seems to be politically correct.

Another problem I've found most magical parents struggle with is that of how to teach spirituality without preaching it. It's easy to become sanctimonious, which turns kids off immediately. In the process of having my children bring *me* up, I've learned that the best answer to this difficulty is exactly what shamanism advocates: simplicity. Find ways to weave your ideals and traditions into everyday activities, and children will learn them by example and through mimicry. Here are some examples and ideas for you to try.

Meal Magic

> *A dining room table with children's eager, hungry faces around it ceases to be a mere dining room table and becomes an altar.*
>
> —Simeon Strunsky

Nearly every herb, food, and beverage on this planet has been categorized at one time or another for its metaphysical abilities. For example, shamans in the East advocate rice for prosperity and abundance. It is also a wishing food on birthdays similar to our Western cakes. So, when your children have a special wish they want to manifest, have them eat rice cakes daily, making that wish mentally as they bite. This literally helps them internalize the energy of the wish for manifestation! When the wish comes true, one rice cake should be given to the earth by way of an offering and gift of thanks.

Among the Native Americans, corn represents providence and blessing. Popcorn symbolizes unexpected guests or good news, and was also frequently used for divination. So, if your child has a pressing need or wants improved perspective, have him or her help you prepare popcorn, cornbread, corn fritters, or other corn dishes. The heat symbolically activates the power of the food. You can also add special chants, songs, and spices to the mixture to accent and augment the magic created. Returning to the illustration of cornbread for perspective, you might offer the idea of adding ginger to the bread for energy and fresh ideas. Then instruct the child to stir the dough clockwise for positive energy while singing a favorite song, which releases joy into the whole procedure.

Here is a list of some foods and beverages and their symbolic attributes from around the world. To this list add any from your own family traditions. For example, examine what you normally eat on specific holidays and why. During this examination you'll likely discover several items that have strong symbolism that can be used magically, and which can be shared with your children while the food is prepared.

FOOD AND BEVERAGE CORRESPONDENCES

Almonds	Sweetness; wealth; love; living presently
Apple	Health; avoiding temptation; peace
Bacon	Financial improvement
Basil	Fire element; power; love
Bay	Protection; prayerfulness; wishes
Beans	Divinatory ability; luck
Berries	Abundance; tribal unity

Birch beer	Banishing negative energies
Bread	Kinship; providence; reconnection
Butter	Success; health
Cabbage	Joyfulness
Cake	Celebration; hope; wishes
Cheese	Love; joy; health
Cherry	Caprice; playfulness
Coconut	Flexibility; thoughtfulness; realness
Cranberry	Safety
Dill	Courage; safety; initiation
Egg	Potential; creativity; integration
Fig	Strength; wisdom; learning; attentiveness
Fish	Providence; deliverance; thankfulness
Garlic	Protection; keeping promises; strength; truthfulness
Ginger	Energy; new ideas; loyalty
Grapes	Celebration; gathering the reward from your work
Honey	Creativity; inspiration; commitment; happiness
Juice	Health; energy
Lemon	Cleansing; love; luck
Meat	Prosperity; abundance
Melon	Love; decision-making
Milk	Fulfillment; self-images; the Mother spirit
Mint	Communication; hospitality; peace
Mushrooms	Leadership; psychic awareness

Oatmeal	Healing; providence
Orange	Well-being; love
Peach	Wisdom; turning away negativity
Pear	Luck
Pineapple	Hospitality; safety; prosperity
Potato	Earth element; health; grounding
Pumpkin	Positive changes
Salt	Honor; endurance; gusto; protection; promises
Soda pop	Joy; happiness; renewed enthusiasm
Soup	Mingling diverse projects or people successfully
Tea	Peace; community; awareness
Tomato	Love
Vanilla	Improving mental abilities; productivity
Watermelon	Good health; friendship
Yogurt	Vitality; spiritual matters

As a case in point, say a child you know is going away to a friend's house for a weekend and he or she is nervous. You might give him or her some mint candies so he or she will be welcome and able to communicate effectively in that setting (note that these are sucked on, releasing the power into the mouth). Or, if a child feels like he or she lacks luck, suggest he or she drinks lemonade daily until things improve. In this way you're sharing some neat metaphysical ideas and empowering that child to begin changing his or her reality.

Prayers

Numerous circumstances give us the opportunity to bring more prayerfulness into our lives and those of our children. Bedtime and mealtime prayers are but two. In our fast-food world, the custom of mealtime prayer has become somewhat passé. Despite this trend it is a tradition that a shamanic lifestyle can resurrect successfully.

At a family dinner, I suggest that each person takes a turn at meal time offering a prayer to the Great Spirit. This prayer should thank both the Creator and the creation for their gifts, and then add anything else for which the family is grateful or has a pressing need. In many Native American traditions, for example, the spirit of the animal being consumed is thanked for its sacrifice. Similarly, vegetarians can thank the plant spirits for their abundance. Children and adults alike should be encouraged to speak from the heart in truthfulness. You'll be amazed at the insights that come from these moments.

At bedtime, children need not kneel in prayer as is traditional in Christian settings. Instead, tell them to do whatever feels right: sing, dance, chant, or just talk. I truly believe that Spirit is far more inclined to heed heartfelt actions and words over rote litany any day.

During prayer, many people (children and adults alike) remember to ask for blessings for their mom, dad, grandma, and the like, but completely forget that they too are important and worthy of blessing. This is a valuable lesson for our youth, who often struggle with self-images and status quo issues. So remind your children to not only give thanks and make requests for others in their prayers, but to also place petitions before the Sacred for themselves, and to talk to Spirit about the things they don't necessarily want to share with anyone else. In a world where everything else changes quickly, god/dess remains an eternal stronghold to which our children can turn for foundations and support anytime.

Quality Time

I know from experience that it's hard to find the kind of time you might wish with your children. During the five years when I was working a full-time job, writing, and lecturing, I found myself scheduling hours of play with my daughter around deadlines, and catching a few moments of the "chase you" game with my son as he passed the computer. Even now that I have simplified my schedule, finding uncommitted blocks of time is quite difficult.

My husband works all day, and finds his level of patience rather thin by the time he gets home. Additionally, once dinner is done, he only has two to three hours before the kids are in bed. By the weekend, both of us are catching up on all the things that didn't get accomplished during the week, and then we try and work in something special for the kids when the chores are done.

We are not the only ones facing these kinds of difficulties and their repercussions. Children often feel left out or bored, or worse yet, turn to the TV for companionship. Adults feel guilty, but can't get out of the work-a-day trap if they want to support the family. Thus we come by the infamous phrase "quality time."

What exactly does quality time mean to a shamanic practitioner? It means living attentively and presently enough so we can give our children love, attention, and insights, whenever and wherever the opportunity strikes. How? Here's some simple illustrations that will hopefully inspire more creative ideas of your own:

- When everyone is doing chores together, sing songs, chant, or make a game out of it. For example, spray floor polish on a cloth and let the kid(s) skate over the wooden surface to clean it while they recite something like: Within I shine, without I shine, soon good luck will be mine! Change the chant to something personally significant for the child.

- When a child complains that he or she is having a bad day, suggest that he or she begins moving clockwise whenever possible. This turns negativity and encourages blessing because it follows the sun's natural movements. Alternatively, suggest the child changes an item of clothing to change luck, or puts on a piece of clothing whose color makes him or her feel better.

- When you pass an animal that's been killed by a car, offer a prayer for the creature's spirit, or ask the child to do it. Explain why if necessary.

- When you're mowing the lawn, make a mandala pattern and explain it to the kids. They can then use this design as a race track; running generates energy for manifestation! If you don't have a lawn, try this with your vacuum cleaner on a plush rug (spiral designs are the easiest in this case).

- When you call the kids in because you're anticipating rain, explain what signs you used to predict it (like the leaves turning, birds singing differently, etc.).

- At bath time, suggest the children pick out one habit or problem they want to wash away, then make up a song or chant to help focus on that goal. When the water is drained, the negativity goes with it!

- At bedtime, encourage the children to use their imaginations to create stories they'd like to dream about (also put a dream catcher over the bed). This improves the child's ability to visualize, and often produces spiritually significant dreams.

- When a child is studying spelling, try a little bibliomancy. Have your child think of a question then randomly open the dictionary and point to a word. See what kind of answer he or she gets, and have the child learn the word too! Likewise, when studying math, teach the child the metaphysical significance of numbers and try a little numerology with his or her birthdate.

These kinds of activities change dramatically depending on the age of the child, your living environment, and personal circumstances. Nonetheless, I think you can see that almost all activities and situations hold the potential for a little magic if viewed with a creative eye. Better still, the more you add exercises and insights like these into your child's life, the more natural it becomes. Eventually you'll find your child following your lead and coming up with ideas all on his or her own. In this manner you also empower your children—empower them to carve out a spiritual path and vision that suits the person they're becoming.

Storytelling

In Shamanic tradition the ethics, values, beliefs, and customs of the tribe are often transmitted to children and outsiders through storytelling. In the tradition of the ancient bard, the shaman memorizes stories from long ago. Some of these stories speak of the spirits, others teach about nature, and still others preserve the tribe's history. No matter the tale, however, the children hearing these stories find a sense of belonging and a heritage in the words that they will carry long into the future.

For your personal storytelling efforts, try making up a story with your child that symbolically deals with something going on in his or her life, or something about which you wish to teach him or her. For example, if your child has been having problems with bullies, you might start a story where someone is facing a fearsome foe, but overcomes the fear somehow. These cooperative tales are fun to try at family gatherings and camping trips too. Here your tribe can sit in a circle with each member contributing something to the creative process.

Alternatively, storytelling time can include tales that you favored as a child, old folk stories, or collections discovered in the library from shamanic cultures around the world. If you're looking for a terrific collection written specifically for children, I highly recommend *In a Circle, Long Ago* (see Bibliography). Look through what you have on hand and try to find a tale that suits the occasion or mood. As you do, don't forget that humor and "just for fun" stories are just as important to children as moralistic tales and histomyths. They release the power of joyfulness into your child's life. Besides, what's really most important about storytelling isn't the exact nature of the tale, it's the time—the private time between you, your child, and the Sacred powers that you allow to pour through your words.

NATURE'S CLASSROOM

In observing nature and its denizens, and in particular the seasonal cycles, wonderful opportunities arise to create a fulfilling spiritual lesson out of nature's classroom. Children have a natural love for the outdoors, so it's very easy to direct their attention to the Earth Mother, especially if you have a fun activity to accompany whatever you're teaching. The following are some ideas that you can try as they stand, or adapt to be more suited to specific age groups.

Animal Mimes

Children have animal totems and guides too, even if they're not consciously aware of them. Performing animal mimes is one way for the child to begin touching those spirits, and connecting more intimately with the animal kingdom. The first experiments with this activity prove most successful if patterned after a family pet or another animal that the child sees and experiences regularly. You can take some time to gather the symbolic information about the chosen creature beforehand, then begin a game of "pretend you're a…" with younger children. As they mimic the animal, ask them how they feel, what they think it would be like to live as that animal, and so forth. Add whatever insights you can that you feel the child will understand.

Around the age of eight, children begin to comprehend much more about spirituality than before, and can be told outright the purpose of such games. In this case, let them choose any animal they want to mimic, and read up on it in a children's encyclopedia or on the computer. Do some breathing exercises with them before they start the mime, and then see what develops. Don't forget to ask questions and talk about the experience afterward, so it has a greater impact.

What's nice about this play-acting is that it gets children to think of animals as more than just play things, but as living creatures like themselves. This understanding and appreciation begins building a lifelong respect for the Mother that will help heal our planet in the future.

Canning and Baking

Earlier in this chapter I discussed magical cookery. Canning and baking during the fall holds similar potential, with two really neat twists. You get to talk about the significance of the season and its crops with your child (a time of thanksgiving and preparation), and the idea of "preserving" the energies you're creating via canning, baking, and freezing. Afterward, have your child help you label the canned or baked goods with fun names that symbolize their magical themes like "joy jam," "thankful tomatoes," and "blessing beans." For more ideas on magical foods, and specifically canning, try reading my book, *The Kitchen Witch's Cookbook* (see Bibliography).

Gardening

Gardening is one of the best ways to get directly in touch with the Mother. Here, children not only learn about natural cycles, but can also begin discovering the metaphysical correspondences for many plants, and they can learn a little of why those associations developed, and how to use that information for manifesting personal goals.

The daisy, for example, has strong solar aspects because it turns its face to follow the sun through the sky, and carrying a daisy is said to draw love to the bearer. So, if a child wants more energy (a solar characteristic), or if he or she hopes to meet more friends, he or she might choose to plant daisies in rich soil with an energized turquoise (for friendship). When the flowers are grown, the child can pick a few flowers, symbolically "gathering in" the magic created by his or her own handiwork.

Other ideas along these lines? How about special rituals to bless the land (or soil) before adding seeds? Plant lavender flowers in gardens, window pots, and indoor planters to sow peace in the home. Add carrots to a vegetable garden so that awareness and spiritual vision can likewise grow. Put some garlic buds at the four elemental corners of the house to protect it. And don't forget harvesting lessons, like giving the plant spirit an offering in thanks, or harvesting a magical herb at summer solstice for greatest power. Really, the possibilities are endless.

Green Plays

Green plays appear in many ancient tribal settings as a way of inspiring abundant harvests and connecting with nature spirits. It's a tremendously fun activity for children of many ages because they get to dress up like flowers, trees, and other plants, and then jump and dance happily so the plants grow and flourish. I personally like using this during early spring rites, having the children make their costumes beforehand out of cardboard, waxed leaves, bits of greenery, scrap fabric, and the like. Inside the sacred circle they then become the plant spirits whose rebirth we honor. Indirectly this encourages continued growth and health for the children too.

Exactly what form the green play takes is really up to you. One fun approach is having the children curl up in tight balls as if sleeping at the outset of the circle. After the invocation, they slowly wake up and spread their petals and leaves to welcome the sunlight. As the light grows throughout the ritual (try having someone turn on extra lights, open curtains, or whatever) the child-plants become more active and joyful, dancing clockwise until it's time to simply sit and bask in the sun's glory. The rest of the ritual continues as normally prescribed by your tradition.

Clean-Up Parties

Earth Day, as most pleasant days throughout the year, provides us with an opportunity to serve the planet. For the shaman, reciprocity with nature is nothing less than essential, and that includes cleaning up human messes. Since children are always looking for a good excuse to go outside and play, you can encourage them to give part of their play time to clean-up projects. For example, in our old neighborhood many walkers often tossed odd bits of trash on people's lawns. Before my son went to play with his friends, he picked these up daily. In our home, recycling is encouraged, so I'm slowly teaching the children how to prepare containers for pickup by the authorities. True, these are small efforts, but every little bit helps, especially when combined with other similar attempts.

Other ideas along these lines include organizing park clean-up days, pollution awareness days, and paper drives (this last effort can raise money for schools or ecological protection groups). Or try holding a contest for neighborhood children to see who can come up with the most creative way of recycling something (break this up by age group). I've found that many businesspeople are happy to contribute small prizes for these kinds of things. Better still, this gets the tribe of your community working and playing together for a greater good.

Feather Finding and Divination

In the previous chapter, I reviewed the idea of the shaman going to nature in search of answers. Feather finding is another such activity perfectly suited to young children. If they randomly find a feather from a particular bird (if it's identifiable), use the opportunity to teach them about that creature's attributes, and any potential message it bears for that child. For example, when we moved into our new home my daughter and I found a white feather, blue feather, and a brown feather together in the backyard. I told her this represented the gifts of peace, joy, and security.

Alternatively, if a child has some pressing questions, he or she can voice that query to the winds, and then go for a walk. Whatever feathers the child finds along the way indicate an answer as follows:

Red	A bit of luck is coming your way
Orange	You'll soon be having some great fun with friends
Yellow	Slow down a bit and be cautious in this situation
Green	A chance to grow or an exciting adventure awaits you
Blue	Peace and unity
Brown	Well-being, especially physical; security
Black	A negative omen, possibly bad news coming
Black and White	Overcoming a problem
Green and Black	Improved finances and reputation
Brown and White	Happiness
Gray and White	Your wish will come true
Blue, White, and Black	A new friend
Purple	A vacation

Wash the found feathers in warm water and keep them. These can be used later in the child's spells, as part of ritual, for smudging, or as decorative additions to walking sticks, power pouches, and medicine shields.

Leaf Pressing and Divination

For a good fall activity, take your child out to find several vari-colored leaves (from as many different species as possible). Twelve is a good number that improves the randomness of this divination method. Take the chosen leaves inside and wax them by placing each leaf between two sheets of waxed paper (wax side facing the leaf) and warming the paper with an iron on a low setting.

Next, have the child place the cooled leaves in a cloth bag, and then randomly draw out a leaf. The interpretation is indicated either by the leaf's color(s) (you can use traditional correspondences or those given for feathers), or by the type of leaf as listed below. Note that these values are written for older children (over the age of eight), so if your child is younger, you may want to change the interpretations to something more appropriate and comprehensible.

Leaf Interpretations

Apple	Improved health or relationships
Ash	Good luck
Aspen	Watch your words
Beech	Make a wish!
Birch	A spirit is trying to get your attention
Cherry	An emphasis on learning
Elder or Elm	Be on the look-out for fairies
Hawthorn	Happiness and fortune will soon be yours, or a chance for a fresh start
Hazel	You will soon find a special treasure
Holly	You will soon have an important dream
Juniper	The dark clouds are lifting, stay hopeful!
Oak	Strength and long life
Poplar	Improved communications
Rose	Love
Rowan and Walnut	Safety, especially from magic
Willow	Self-control or improved psychic insights

Note: For greater durability you can laminate or decoupage the waxed leaves.

Moon Calendars

In Chapter 2, I discussed designing a personal moon calendar and finding a way to honor that calendar as part of your regular mini-rituals. Children can follow suit, but you'll probably have to help them create the calendar and associated observances. In fact, I really encourage making this a partnered activity so your child knows that you respect his or her vision and ideas.

Names for each month's moons might derive from the weather, activities, special events in the child's life, and so forth. Activities can vary from year to year to reflect the child's age and growing understanding. Additionally, if a child feels the need to alter his or her moon names in accordance with maturity, he or she should be encouraged to do so. Shamanism advocates external transformations in one's practices that mirror what's happening internally.

Stone Messages

During nature walks, a day in the park, or any other moments outdoors, children often find neat stones that they want to bring home as personal treasures. When this happens it's the perfect time to discuss the energy housed by each stone, and its gift to us as a witness to much of human history. You can then examine the color or patterns on the stone with the child (similarly to the system presented in the "Findings" section in Chapter 6) to see if nature was providing a message.

Once the stone is home it can go on the child's altar, be placed on a talking/walking stick, become part of a power pouch, get blessed and used as a portable amulet or charm, or even perhaps get woven into her or his personal dream catcher.

Sandcastle Wishing

My children love the water and will swim and play literally until they turn blue from the cold. This is quite natural considering we spend nine months of our pre-birth time in a watery environment. And since most children seem memorized by the beach, you can add a little magic to the day's adventure by teaching about the significance of tides (which tie into the moon) and how to use them for wishing.

The Norse, for example, feel that the time of day when the tide arrives changes its energy. A morning tide is good for wishes pertaining to energy, new ideas, and attentive living. A day tide helps with growth, money, and connection. A midday tide brings providence and strength, and an evening tide creates energy for joy and realness. Night tides hold creativity and knowledge. Midnight tides help with healing wishes, and pre-morning tides are good for thoughtfulness and rest.

To utilize these ideas, just suggest that the child find a biodegradable symbol of his or her wish and bury it in the sand during the right tide. When the emblem gets washed out to sea (or lake) it caries the wish with it. Alternatively, the child can build a symbolic sandcastle for the tide to wash away, slowly dispersing the wish energy he or she places within!

Sign and Omen Observation

Chapter 6 provides a brief list of natural omens and signs. Teaching these to children is fairly easy and fun for them too. For example, I now have my son listening to birds, observing ants, and checking the winds to try and predict storms and other weather patterns. For him it's a game; for me it's a game that builds his observation skills and awareness of the earth.

Start with easily remembered things, and mention them as a side comment during your conversations. For example, the old saying of "red sun at morning" is a good mnemonic device because it rhymes (nearly all scholastic systems teach younger children through rhymes). So if you're planning a day out with your child, and you notice a reddish sun, you can tell him or her the rhyme and bring an umbrella!

This slowly integrates nature's lore into the way our children respond to the world, and encourages earth-friendly behavior. It also teaches them that there is much to life that goes slightly beyond normal awareness, some of which can be discovered just by looking a little more closely. In this lesson, the first seeds of magical thinking can be planted in our children's hearts—thinking that allows for limitless possibilities.

Talking and Walking Stick

In Chapter 2, in the section on ritual components, I discussed the use of a talking stick as part of rites. For children, I suggest fallen branches over commercially made staffs for two reasons. First, the commercial ones are often chemically treated. Second, a branch your child finds on a special outing with you will have more meaning for him or her.

Before trying to find a talking stick, you may want to have the child sit beneath a tree and meditate or pray. This attunes the child to the tree spirits' voices. Even a brief pause to breathe and focus before the search will help the child find just the right staff: one that provides support, improves communication, and guides his or her feet surely along the Path of Beauty.

Once found and decorated with personally significant items (feathers, stones, drawings or whatever), the staff can be used in ritual to call the quarters. It can become a magic wand for directing energy, and a walking stick for nature hikes. Most importantly, it becomes the child's talking stick both in and out of the circle.

For the last function, tell your child that whenever he or she needs to talk to you about something, your child should leave the staff in a special spot. I've found that it's much easier for children to make a symbolic gesture (placing the stick) than it is to confront

adults directly with their needs. The stick acts as a silent signal between the two of you, to which you will immediately respond to help
your child with whatever is on his or her mind.

☾

There are certainly far more nature-inspired activities than
those given here. Think back to your own childhood. What kinds of
things did you enjoy doing outdoors? Did you weave flowers into
caplets, wheat or corn into braids, or have leaf-raking parties?
Believe it or not, your children will likely enjoy similar things, to
which you can add a magical dimension. When weaving flowers, add
a chant for happiness and beauty; with corn or wheat, pray for providence. When gathering leaves, sing a song of what you want to
gather into your life. Look at each moment of living as an opportunity to teach nature's lessons and the ways of the shaman to your
child, through recognition, joyfulness, thankfulness, and love.

SHAMANIC GAMES

Tribal cultures were often more clever than modern-minded folk
give them credit for. They found fun ways of teaching children spiritual principles and talents through play. Many games in Native
American and other shamanic traditions have layers of intention,
only one of which is purely pleasurable or competitive. The following are a couple of examples that you can try with your own children.

The Bone Game

At its core, the bone game is an exercise that improves psychic awareness. Traditionally two people or two teams play this game ceremoni-
ally, each taking turns hiding a marked bone. In a team setting, one
person is usually designated as a "seer." It is this person's job to become
a kind of spiritual pointer or dowsing rod to uncover the bone. The
seer, or the seer and the team, devise a strategy for doing just that.

The other player/team then does everything they can to prevent the seer from discovering the bone's hiding place using techniques like glamoury, auric shielding, and the like. The opposing team can also dance, mimic their power animals, or make animal sounds to try and distract the seer's resolve. Many players often carry quartz crystals with them for good luck.

Group settings seem to offer the greatest instructional potential in that the team must learn to merge their magic into one cone of power that will seek out the bone or keep it hidden. This takes time and patience to master, and teaches both children and adults how to better use auric energy.

There are several different adaptations of this game appearing in widely disparate regions. Sometimes more than one object is used for the game, each of which has a different value. The hope here is that the seer will be distracted by the energies of the other objects over the prized bone. Sometimes items are hidden in moccasins or mittens. Various types of beans might be secured in reeds, or balls placed under carved cups. All this leads me to believe that the modern shell game developed from these sources.

Hoop Games

See far around you.

—Ojibwe elder

In Chapter 2, I discussed the symbolic importance of the circle in core shamanism. The circle represents creation, the Creator, the vision of truth, the Medicine Wheel, the ever-extending universe, far-reaching possibilities, and balance. The sacred circle is forever moving us toward destiny, toward reunion with Spirit. Hoop games stress these meanings, sometimes taking the form of a dance, and sometimes taking the form of a dart game.

In the hoop dance, a child is encouraged to move in a personal way, mimicking the circle somehow through his or her body. Older children are actually given small colored hoops to dance with, like partners in an elaborate version of the hoola hoop. The goal is to add as many hoops as possible into the dance, and to design the hoops intricately so they mirror the web of life, the common bonds of the human tribe, and the patterns of the universe.

Among the Plains Indians in particular, a total of twenty-eight hoops are used to represent the lunar cycle. An accomplished hoop dancer can tell stories with the hoops and turn them into all manners of visual images, including that of a butterfly. But what's best about the hoop dance is that there is no "right" or "wrong" way to enact it. A child can truly express himself or herself and have fun, while also reconnecting with important symbols and ideas.

The second type of hoop game begins with a circle of intertwined branches, some of which are decorated very similarly to a dream catcher. This represents the web of life, spun by Spider Woman. To this, some long, sharpened feathers or corncobs are added. Players for this game, which appears in tribes as diverse as the Hopi and Zuni, aim their darts at the circle, which is rolled along the ground clockwise following the sacred wheel.

The symbolism here of hitting one's mark in the circle of life should not be overlooked. Beyond the symbolism, however, there was a very practical application for this game in hunting. It honed a person's aim. With this in mind, the game could have been used as part of pre-hunting rituals as a type of magical mimicry—several successful hits portended a likewise successful hunt. For our purposes this might be part of a spell for children in which they help themselves achieve specific goals by putting energy into the dart (the throw) and hitting the bull's eye.

OTHER PROJECTS AND ACTIVITIES

Children seem to have an inexhaustible supply of energy. Consequently, shamanic parents need to be prepared with clever projects

194

and activities to fill the ever-hungry young mind and spirit. Here are five activities that you can try or adapt.

Children's Altars

If your child shows a natural interest in, and leaning toward, shamanism, he or she can make a special altar to honor that decision. Children's altars can be very flexible in their construction. Use the top of a toy box, a book shelf, part of a closet, or whatever, as a base. As to what goes on the altar, that's up to your child. Found feathers, stones, flowers, favorite toys, pictures of loved ones—anything he or she treasures, anything that reminds him or her to be the best person he or she can be—is appropriate here.

While it might be tempting to meddle, I really suggest a "hands-off" policy for yourself and other members of your household on this one. The young shaman's altar should reflect his or her vision, *not* yours. Besides, you'll find that a child's sensitivity often lends itself to some pretty amazing altars that honor the Sacred in ways that you never considered.

Fire Scrying and Candle Control

Fire fascinates most people, no matter their age. For thousands of years tribes have gathered around fires for safety, cooking, and ritual. As nature's element for change, energy, power, illumination, and cleansing, fire holds great import to shamans who consider it the most difficult element to master.

Fire scrying is one activity that helps build your child's ability to concentrate and focus, and begins establishing his or her relationship with this tricky element (and thereby building respect for it, too). During the summer months when you're camping or sitting at a bonfire, begin talking about the salamanders who live in the flames and how they can hear our questions. During winter, the same concept can be discussed any time you light a candle, or even when you're cooking on a gas stove. Note, however, that you should always stress the importance of having adult supervision for this exercise.

Next, teach your child how to pose a question, perhaps by tossing in special herbs or just by whispering to the flames (carefully). Tell him or her to watch the fire, but not directly, and to look for specific signs. Bright, dancing flames are a positive response. Small, dull flames mean "no," and if the fire goes out it's a negative sign.

An alternative to fire scrying is learning the art of candle control. This is a very simple exercise that *must* be supervised for safety, but it's an excellent one for teaching your children focus and auric management. Sit in front of a candle with the child and have him or her hold his or her hand about one foot away from it either to the left or right. Next, instruct the child to think about the energy around the body: specifically, he or she should try and push it out toward the candle. When the flame moves away from his or her hand, the child has successfully manipulated his or her own aura.

Over time my son has learned how to make the flame grow, shrink, and dance with greater aptitude than many of my adult students. In the process he's gained an abiding respect for this element, having seen firsthand that one does not "play" with fire. Additionally, he's begun to show a growing relationship with the salamanders that will benefit him in the years ahead.

Pinwheel Prayers

Pinwheels are a terrific toy that can become a makeshift Medicine Wheel for your child. Simply buy a pinwheel and have him or her write words or short phrases on each quarter that represent needs, wishes, and other prayers to Spirit. Older children can use symbolic colors or drawings, too. Then, they can put the pinwheel where it receives wind (possibly coming from the right elemental direction to emphasize the goal(s)). Each time the pinwheel turns, it represents a prayer being released. Or, if the need is more pressing, the child can blow on the wheel to release the magic and give it life (symbolized by breath).

If you can't find a pinwheel, alternatives include flying small cloth swatches painted with symbols from a tree, flying a kite with similarly symbolic images on it, and/or releasing flower petals to the winds with a prayer.

Shaman's Sphere

This is a neat project for the holidays, as the spheres make wonderful decorations and gifts. Begin with any see-through globe that can be opened (you can buy these at craft shops). Give your child a mixture of stones, feathers, herbs, and other items that he or she can choose for filling the globe. The fillings should have symbolic value, such as lavender for joy, a turquoise stone for health, and a red feather for luck.

After filling one-half of the globe, help the child glue it together, and then add decorations on the outside. Nice additions include little ribbons tied with bells, beads, glitter, and the like. The child can then hang the finished sphere in a window, off a rearview mirror in the car, on the Yule tree, in her or his room, or give it to someone as a gift.

Wish and Dream Nets

A youthful version of a dream catcher, wish and dream nets are made from any convenient netting (such as a fisherman's net, or even bug netting). To the net, the child can attach little bundles of goodies that represent what he or she most wish for and want to dream about. By connecting a symbolic token with the net, the child helps draw the energy necessary for manifestation along life's network. Here are a few ideas for items that can tie into the net:

SYMBOLIC TOKENS

Bark	Strength and protection
Charms (like those from bracelets)	Wishes and hopes

Crystal Beads	Clarity, energy, and diversity
Feathers	Joy and lightheartedness
Flowers	Beauty and self-confidence
Greeting Cards	Love and good wishes
Herb Bundles	Varies with the herb's metaphysical correspondence
Key Chain Animals (stuffed)	The child's totem(s)
Paperdolls	Our tribes (especially if connected at the hands)
Photographs	Prayers for those depicted in the picture
Ribbon	Holding energy in place until its needed (untie one ribbon when they want that attribute to manifest)
Rings or Hoops	Cycles, the sacred circle
Toys (small)	Depends on the item. For example, a set of keys can represent opportunity or openings.

Once completed, hang this dream net from the ceiling in the child's room by hooks so that it is over his or her bed or altar. This is also a nice decorative item for playrooms. Note: For children who have a fear of the dark, I recommend making your own netting out of glow-in-the-dark string, available at novelty shops. The pale light won't keep them awake and it inspires security, which naturally brings better dreams.

CHILDREN IN RITUAL

There seems to be a lot of discussion about the propriety of having children in the sacred circle. As representations of our future, however, I cannot imagine a circle without them. The beauty of watching magical children in a ritual setting came to me firsthand at a recent gathering. I was sitting near a bardic fire watching children taking turns telling stories, and dancing merrily with the salamanders. Their movements were so natural, so sensitive, and so filled with life's power. I was completely awestruck, and terribly moved by the whole experience. In that moment I saw what our children can become when brought up with magic as a natural part of life.

I will be the first to agree that there are *some* rituals unsuited to young attendants. Whenever such occasions arise, perhaps children can participate at the opening of a circle, and then go for lessons elsewhere during the body of ritual, a separation akin to Sunday school. Alternatively, we can create rituals designed especially for younger participants. For example, a coming-of-age ritual might be created and performed by other members of your tribe who have recently come of age themselves. This way they start learning what it is like to be an adult member of the group, and the new adult member is greeted by his or her peers.

Another good example comes from Chippewa tradition. It is a ritual simply called "first dance," and it celebrates the first time a child joins the ritual circle wearing appropriate garb. At this ritual, each child participating is anointed with berries for life's sweetness, and honored by the calling of his or her name. Within this space, children aren't directed, but are left to Spirit's leadings on what form his or her dance takes: the drum guides them; the fire guides them; the joy guides them. This symbolizes the fact that each person makes his or her own path in life, and also within the sacred circle.

ADVICE FROM SPIRIT

I can't say that raising a child in a neo-shamanic tradition is easy, but it is worthwhile. When you find yourself uncertain about what concepts to share, how to share them, or what activities to try, don't forget that you need not feel alone in this task. Both Spirit and your totems can help.

Before approaching your children about a difficult magical concept or ideal, return to the world tree and ask for aid. Watch what your power animal does, where it goes, or listen to its words. Climb to the top of the tree and look out over the cosmos. Somewhere in the shrewdness of the spirit animal, or the songs of the Ancients, you will find the wisdom to teach your children what they most need now, and what will remain with them for the rest of their lives.

sacred ground: honoring the earth

The beauty of the trees, the softness of air, the
fragrance of the grass, speaks to me…
and my heart soars.

—Chief Dan George

The shaman is a warrior priest. In this case the "good fight" is one aimed at reclaiming the sanctity of our planet and renewing a close human relationship with all of nature's spirits. This chapter, therefore, discusses ways to reconnect with and honor the earth, no matter where you live.

I have chosen to focus most of this writing on building a positive relationship with the Mother and helping to heal Her, rather than on the negatives. Enough has been said about ecology, pollution, and the raping of the earth's resources to understand what has already taken place. The past cannot be undone. The future, however, is well within the shaman's grasp.

If we begin to live today, in this moment, living in harmony with nature and all its creatures…if we grow to cherish nature and its creatures, then we can begin spiritually re-landscaping the earth using love as our guide.

A SHAMAN'S WORLDVIEW

> *See the Self in every creature and all creation in*
> *the Self.*
>
> —Bhagavad Gita (6:28–32)

Everything in nature has a soul or spirit worthy of respect, including the planet. Consequently, the way a shaman approaches all aspects of living on the earth is different than many other people's approach. He or she does not disregard nature's signals or cries for aid, and gives all living things due courtesy.

This respectful attitude becomes very apparent when observing any shamanic gathering of ritual components from the land. Wherever a tree is cut for firewood, for example, small tokens like fruits or nuts are left behind as gifts. Before even touching that tree, the shaman offers a prayer of apology and thanks the tree for its gifts. Through these kinds of thoughtful actions the shaman honors the earth, even when what's under his or her feet is concrete.

A shamanic worldview can be summed up by saying that the shaman:

- Appreciates the earth in all its forms

- Recognizes that he or she is not superior to any other living thing in the great scheme of life's network

- Experiences the earth as intimately as possible

- Regards the earth as something under his or her protection

- Works within natural laws, in partnership with the earth, both on temporal and spiritual levels

- Behaves kindly toward the earth and its creatures

- Strives to reunify himself or herself with the earth's spirit and that of all living things

- Endeavors to inspire an awakening of earth-awareness in others and to help repattern negative behaviors

- Trusts in the earth's ability to provide for us if we treat it properly

Appreciation and intimate experience provides the shaman with the awareness and motivation necessary to become a contentious caretaker. Stewardship fosters responsible action, and this doesn't just mean in the physical sense. It also means making sure that one's magical/spiritual efforts always flow within natural laws and guidelines. Why? Because the shaman is building an all-important relationship with nature's spirits. Most good relationships begin with attention to detail and genuine admiration. When you feel this way, it's all but impossible to purposefully step outside the lines of what's considered "white" magic.

Union brings a broadening of one's horizons, both above and below. When you are one with earth, you are one with creation. There is no difference, no division, between you and a bluebird, you and a hill, or you and a star, other than those divisions that you impose. Anytime such oneness occurs it opens the heart and spirit in amazing ways. It creates a new clarity, a fresh appreciation for all that is, was, and will be. It creates thankful living.

Appreciation also leads the shaman to sharing his or her vision enthusiastically with others, inspiring a fresh vision. This doesn't mean peddling ecological journals on the street corner. Remember: Urban shamanism doesn't advocate browbeating. Instead, the shaman strives to find simple ways to inspire and manifest change.

Finally, the shaman wholeheartedly trusts that if he or she continues to live gently with the earth, the planet will provide for his or her needs. This creates a "give away" approach to life. Shamans give of what they have to others in need, believing that providence is a gift to be shared. Compare this ideology with the "take away" society in which we live, that keeps taking and hoarding until nothing is left. You can see how it might be difficult for some people to integrate or understand a shamanic worldview. This seems especially true of Westerners who have grown accustomed to success-oriented and profit-oriented thinking.

Nonetheless, the shaman has the power to change old, outmoded thought patterns, and to begin building ones that are more positive and life-affirming both for himself or herself and the world. The transformation process need not be a solitary quest. You have Spirit and your totems standing by to help. You also can call on the aid of animal, stone, and plant wisdom to guide and teach you in awakening the shaman's worldview within.

Animal Wisdom

Earlier in this book I discussed the importance of natural and spiritual animals in shamanic practices. Viewing animals as more than allies in this world or in the astral landscape, a shaman respects all creatures because they are part of his or her family, part of creation's tribe, part of earth's classroom, and part of the greater classroom of the cosmos. Consequently, all animals are worthy of the shaman's esteem.

Shamans show this reverence in numerous ways. In some settings the shaman might consult animal wisdom to help in healing or to predict the weather. In another, a hunted animal will receive prayers and offerings to thank its spirit and to give the creature peace. Some ancient myths even depict the earth itself as a great animal, such as a turtle or buffalo. With these examples in mind, animal wisdom becomes very important to our efforts to reconnect with the earth and awaken the shaman within. Animals already live in harmony with nature and they know earth's cycles—it's not something they have to stop and think about; it's instinctive.

An excellent example of the shamanic trust in animal wisdom comes from studies done by Alfonso Ortiz, a noted anthropologist, on the Chippewa tribe in Canada. A medicine man of the tribe insisted that the local surveyors had picked a bad location for a dam. When asked about his assertion, the shaman replied that since no beavers were using that earth, then it was obvious that the land was no good for human dams either. Scientific testing proved the shaman correct. Here animal wisdom allowed him to make a quick, accurate judgment that had taken engineers weeks to complete!

Other than through observation and study, how can one come to know animal wisdom? Many old shamanic stories tell of a time when people were much closer to the animal world. In fact, there was a time when the affiliation was so close that humans communicated freely with animals. Exactly what form this communication took isn't clear. It may have been verbal, empathic, or through some type of mimicry. Whatever the form, the knowledge seems to have been lost over the ages.

Today, some individuals report minor instances of communication happening between an animal and themselves. These reports frequently center around a beloved pet who somehow lets its owner know that something's wrong, or where a missing item lies, or who seems to understand its owner's needs. These experiences give us reason to hope that our ability to understand animal wisdom hasn't been totally erased. To return to a more complete two-way rapport, however, will require a change in attitude. We will have to start regarding animals, once thought of as inferior, as being worthy of our attention.

Each creature is a spirit like us housed in a temporary form— a spirit with insights to share if we but stop and listen. Among the most important of these insights is how to live presently, in this moment, totally at peace with self. Our animal cousins do not fret over the past or what hasn't happened yet; they do not strive to be like one another. They simply live now, content with the form that Spirit gave them.

Another way of gaining animal wisdom is through middle world journeys. Here, spirit animals can instruct us on numerous things, including ways to better understand and unite with the earth. Exactly which animal you call upon to assist you depends greatly on what you want to learn, do, or change in yourself. Someone seeking to strengthen his or her ties to all of life's network, for example, would do well to call on the spider spirit for aid.

ANIMAL CORRESPONDENCES

Ant	Transmuting "dirt" into something productive (e.g., recycling). Cultivating a wise partnership with the earth in working toward its betterment.
Badger	Integrating the strength or aggressiveness with which to protect the earth and its resources.
Bat	Adapting your earth-centered thinking and efforts to changing times and new technology or knowledge that becomes available.
Bear	Initiating a leadership role in any earth-centered effort confidently.
Beaver	Using sensibility and resourcefulness in taking from the earth, building on it, or working with it.
Buffalo	Strengthening the intimacy of your relationship with earth's spirit (or nature spirits).
Cougar	Finding mystical approaches for reunification and earth healing.
Crow	Learning how to shapeshift into different animals to uncover their wisdom.
Deer	Walking gently on the earth in the spirit of prayerfulness and thanksgiving.

Dog	Staying true to your convictions with regard to earth, even when circumstances make it difficult.
Dolphin	Working effectively and joyfully with earth's water resources and water animals.
Eagle	Recognizing earth-friendly approaches or perspectives for a perplexing problem.
Fox	Mastering clever survival skills so you can learn to "give away" rather than "take away."
Frog	Identifying concrete ways in which to cleanse and replenish the earth.
Hawk	Improving your ability to work psychically with animals, minerals, or plants.
Horse	Accepting your power to make a difference and get things moving.
Lizard	Meeting animal guides in dream time for teaching.
Lynx	Understanding nature's hidden messages and secrets. Receiving visions or omens from nature, and gaining knowledge from same.
Mouse	Reassessing your life, especially the small details, to see where earth-friendly changes can be made and waste eliminated.
Otter	Seeing the world with the hopefulness and joy of a child. Not being overly bound to material things, so you can "give away."
Porcupine	Freeing yourself from an over-emphasis on the work-a-day world long enough to enjoy nature's simple beauties.
Rabbit	Overcoming negative or defeatist attitudes when considering the planetary state.

Snake	Understanding nature's cycles and how they affect us. Seeing the earth as a sacred space. Nonverbal communication with animals.
Spider	Strengthening your ties to earth, and helping you to network with other like-minded people.
Thunderbird	Becoming a guardian of earth's truths and lessons, and a fervent preserver of its resources.
Turtle	Putting down firm roots in the earth, stabilizing that relationship, and renewing your respect for all living things.
Whale	Developing a good balance between physical and spiritual efforts to reconnect with and heal the earth. Not repeating past mistakes.
Wolf	Teaching others what you have learned of animal wisdom (or other lessons from nature's classroom).

Please realize that these associations have been limited to associations that directly relate to earth-centered efforts, and are generalizations at best. Exactly what message a spirit animal has for you can be totally unique to your circumstances and environment. Remain open, presume nothing, and receive.

To apply animal wisdom in a variety of settings, the shaman often ritually adds animal parts to fetishes and medicine bundles. This process evokes a creature's attributes and powers, conferring them to the bearer. For example, someone wishing to increase his or her awareness of animals with strong lunar affiliations might carry an owl feather or a rabbit's foot as part of a bundle. Both creatures are metaphysically associated with the moon's energy.

Fetishes and medicine bundles are considered a powerful gift from nature, and they often came with a taboo attached. For example, someone wishing to remain safe from drowning might carry a snippet of beaver fur, but at no time could he or she exhibit a fear or disdain of water. To do so would insult the beaver's spirit, who loves this element, and would thereby decrease or destroy the fetish's potency.

If you wish to make a power pouch or fetish for yourself, I suggest either using a carving or picture of the creature, or a part that you find in nature and that you clean properly. In the first instance you're providing a creative substitute that's earth-friendly. In the second, you're accepting a gift from nature, but also taking precaution against disease.

I have a friend who takes this whole idea one step further. She gathers up road kill, releases the animal's spirit through prayers and offerings, cleans the skins, then makes power pouches using every part of the creature possible. In this manner an animal's life that would have otherwise been wasted becomes a blessing. This is one of the best examples I've seen of a shamanic worldview in action.

Stone Wisdom

In the shamanic worldview, rocks are alive in their own way. While moving far more slowly than other things on earth, they patiently sit, watching. In this manner, stone wisdom connects us to our ancient tribal past and all of human history. Perhaps it is from them that we can learn not to make the same mistakes twice.

Rocks teach us much about strength and security. It was from rocks that some of the first altars and homes were built. To this day, a special cornerstone often marks a home or building as if lending its stability to the whole area. This kind of practical and symbolic value was not lost on early shamans. All types of stones were added to shamanic arts nearly from day one. For example, unremarkable stones got added to the pile for a sweatlodge ceremony. Their wisdom and power comes from being able to hold and radiate heat.

Quartz is very popular shamanic stone, having been used for dreaming, healing, luck-giving, and divining. It may, in fact, be the most utilitarian of all crystals for shamanic work. Many tribal societies, including those of Australia and South Africa, considered quartz a living rock because of its spiritual radiance. Today, science recognizes that quartz does, indeed, generate energy. So, when you first begin studying stone wisdom, quartz is certainly an excellent option to explore.

Science has also kindly shown us other things about stone wisdom that the clever urban shaman can easily apply. Copper, for example, directs energy. It then becomes an excellent addition to a talking stick or a fetish bag, for when you want power to go somewhere specific. Lodestone attracts energy of a specific type, so it's a good component to any charms for drawing what you most desire to you.

How does one go about finding the right stone for the right application? Begin by consulting a good metaphysical correspondence list, but don't stop there. A stone's color, size, facets, and environment all affect what wisdom and powers it has. A book can't predict or portray these quirks; that's for your insight to determine.

Once you do find a suitable stone, mineral, or crystal, it will need some care and pampering to function best as a teacher and shamanic ally. Follow these guidelines to keeping your stone's power active, ample, and working as needed:

- Cleanse and bless the stone in any manner suited to your tradition and its purpose.

- Find a protective covering for the stone. This should be made from a natural fabric, fur, feathers, soft leaves or flower petals, moss, or leather. Replace the leaves, flowers, and/or moss regularly for suppleness.

- Do not show this power object to anyone unless the stone spirit instructs it. To do so is considered a show of vanity, and it insults the stone spirit.

- Regularly feed your crystal by placing it in sunlight, moonlight, water, soil, or whatever seems most suitable for at least three days. For the urban shaman who gets bombarded with ongoing negativity that depletes the stone's power, do this quarterly (minimally)—at the spring and fall equinoxes and during summer and winter solstices. The elemental mediums and the timing suggested both recharge the stone's figurative battery. Your stone's spirit will let you know if it needs a boost before the regularly scheduled maintenance time.

• In moments when you want to release a little extra stone wisdom into a particular situation, rub the stone on your body. For example, when you feel flighty or light-headed, rub yourself with a grounding stone like hematite or obsidian. The static created by rubbing carries the energy to your aura.

Alternatively, if you want the stone's power to radiate away from you, tap the stone lightly on a rock three times, then turn it to face the desired direction. This creates a vibration, releasing the energy desired. Do not, however, do this with all your might. Breaking the crystal is considered a terrible omen, which is often followed by a loss of personal power.

Shamanism offers many ways for you to apply stone wisdom to your daily practices. Meditate with a specially chosen stone on your third eye for insight (perhaps fluorite), or on your chakras for healing (i.e., bloodstone, coral, or carnelian). Put one under your pillow (i.e., silver, amethyst, or azurite) to encourage prophetic or spiritual dreams. Use them for pendulum work, wear them for increased vitality, put them in medicine bundles, on dream catchers, and on your altar.

As a side note, several shamans I know who work regularly with stone wisdom have reported some interesting results. Specifically, when local disasters came their way, such as an earthquake or a tornado, their houses stayed firm while those of neighbors were destroyed. While I cannot prove this had anything to do with these people's ongoing relationships with stone spirits, it certainly didn't hurt!

Plant Wisdom

Listen patiently, quietly, and reverently to the lessons, one by one, which mother nature has to teach, shedding light on that which was before a mystery.

—Luther Burbank

Some people find it hard to think of plants as having any other messages for humankind other than "Water me." Yet the shaman sees all inhabitants of the plant kingdom as spirits to honor, appease, and to observe for insights and lessons. In nearly all shamanic traditions studied, the medicine person has turned to the plant world to expand consciousness through its unique medicine. By internalizing sacred mushrooms, peyote, cactus, tobacco, or herbs, the shaman breaks the barriers of consciousness, and embarks on trance journeys, most often of a very significant or urgent nature.

Note that partaking of the chosen plant is but one part of a complex ritual that often begins months or even years before that day. Sacred plants are ritually planted, ritually grown, ritually harvested, and ritually prepared. At no step along the way is the end product considered suitable for recreation or "kicks." To abuse a plant's wisdom for personal gain or a mere rush insults the spirit, and usually results in a very negative experience.

Before consumption, the shaman prepares himself or herself by bathing, fasting, abstaining from specific foods or sex, and/or other similar purifying efforts. Such efforts cleanse the body, release the spirit, and purify motivations. They also act as a mini-ritual that prepares the shaman's mind to move away from temporal constraints and overcome any obstacles between herself or himself and a successful spirit encounter.

Urban shamans might find it difficult to internalize plant wisdom in traditional ways because of legalities. But, if you should embark on such a venture, please do so following these sensible guide-lines:

- Do so only if you can approach the act as a sacrament in which you will commune intimately with a plant teacher.

- Wait until a time when you are truly whole in body, mind, and spirit. Any good guide will tell you that physical weakness, mental insecurity, or spiritual blemishes can drastically tarnish the experience or turn it into a nightmare.

- Read up on your options, the plant's effects, any side effects, and any allergy tendencies. Just because this is a spiritual effort, don't forego your mind and reason.

- Go to the middle realm of the world tree and introduce yourself to that plant's spirit before any ritual involving that plant. If you can't find it, ask your animal totem to help you. Take time getting to know that energy and make yourself one with it.

- Find someone who is considered a master of that plant. Have this person instruct you on the proper preparation for what you're about to undertake, and follow his or her directions to the letter.

- Ask your totem animals and spirit guides to stand watch over you during the rite.

It is *not* "necessary" to use sacred plants in learning about plant wisdom. Nature kindly provides us with several other alternatives. Gardening is one. Here we have a truly hands-on way of getting close to plant spirits. Gardening's ability to connect with plant spirits is seen in various traditional rites.

During the spring certain Native American shamans dig clock-wise in a plot of land from the center outward. This prepares the pregnant earth, which in turn will nurture the plant spirits being sown. Similarly, come fall, the first harvest is accompanied by a first food or flowering ritual. This is where you thank the land for its gifts through an offering to the plant spirits. Such a ritual is said to ensure ongoing abundance this season and the next.

These two examples provide the green-thumbed urban shaman with abundant material for adaptation. You might be working with window boxes and pots instead of a tract of land, but the effect is the same, especially when combined with personally meaningful touches. During the spring, for example, consider adding a soil blessing, putting energized crystals in the soil, or sowing seed during propitious astrological phases. Choose plants that you can accommodate considering your space, and those that will be most useful to your practices.

And, for those of you who talk or sing to your plants, keep doing so! In fact, sing to them! Chant to them! Plant growth and abundance have been scientifically shown to improve when human emotions and input are literally upbeat. This response indicates the plant spirit is responding to you. I personally think this is a terrific way to raise your magical herbs for incense, strewing, etc. By the time you harvest them, your spirit will be attuned to the plant and any associated devic entities like fairies, and the plant will be saturated with your positive energy.

A second way of touching base with plant spirits is through nature's symbols. Throughout history, every bit of greenery on this world has been given symbolic, healthful, and magical correspondences that you can study, ponder, and/or apply. In many settings, for example, the tree represents the spiritual duties of a shaman: to be well rooted; to stay flexible and grow with the earth's changes; to honor both the past and the future—the above and below. The bark, fruit, or roots of that tree might get used in healing preparations, as part of ritual incense, as spell components, in the communal fires, and in power pouches, just to name a few, In this way, plant teachers meet us on both the esoteric and very practical levels.

No matter what your approach, plant wisdom is vitally important to our world today. It is through nature's citizens that we can learn how to cultivate crops in difficult areas, increase yields, forestall the extinction of various species, and generally begin making progress toward the regreening of the planet.

NATURE'S TEMPLES

> *Behold, a sacred voice is calling you. All over*
> *the sky a sacred voice is calling.*
>
> —Sioux song

While all of creation is hallowed ground, there are some places that seem more special than others—places that radiate an ambiance that speaks of timeless power and potential. Whenever possible, these are the places that a shaman seeks out to augment and empower his or her practice. To do so, however, one must first know what to look for.

Patterns of Power

The ancients built temples, wells, megaliths, and other important structures along what seem to be an invisible energy network. In old England a bright line of grass was called a fairy path. The grass was believed to have thrived when these nature spirits passed by. Modernly, the New Age movement has restored interest in these external testimonies to earth's power grid through sacred geometry and the study of ley lines.

In trying to understand ley lines, think of the earth as if it were a human body. This body has an aura, but it is one that goes far beyond the human dimension, reaching ever outward into space. Just like in human bodies, whenever the earth's body gets injured, its aura also suffers, causing the disruption or destruction of many ley lines, power centers, and vortexes. On a social level, these disruptions become a little more tangible: crime, drug abuse, apathy, and many other social illnesses originate in part with the earth's astral distress. This is why I believe that humankind will never find true wholeness until we begin healing the earth in body and spirit.

To define things a little further, ley lines create the earth's life-network both on the ground and in the air. This means that a shaman can direct his or her magic like electricity neatly along these lines to where it's intended. Overall, this is a far more efficient use of energy, decreasing the strain on the shaman dramatically.

Power centers usually develop where ley lines intersect, but they can develop in regions for other reasons too, usually because it's a site of religious or historical importance. A vortex is quite similar, except that the energy at that spot is in motion, spinning around a nucleus, making a natural cone of power. Power centers and vortexes augment the shaman's natural abilities geometrically, especially when the regional elemental/metaphysical theme mirrors the shaman's goals.

Knowing all this, and seeing the advantages to spending time in such power spots, the next obvious question becomes: How does one find sacred places and power centers?

Finding Sacred Space

When someone asks you to name a sacred place, you'll probably immediately answer with one of the "biggies," such as Stonehenge or the Pyramid at Giza. In reality, however, many power centers of the world have no name whatsoever, and some are yet to be uncovered. They exist in wells, stone outcroppings, a majestic old oak, a waterfall, on farms, in city apartments, and even perhaps in your own backyard. Even so, you may have never tried to find such a place, not knowing exactly what to look for. If this is the case, here are some guidelines for recognizing power centers. Look for a region where:

- You sense a presence or power that is inescapable. I've only experienced this once in my life, in a little chapel deep in a castle. The minute I walked across the threshold the holiness of that place was almost audible. While there, I couldn't bring myself to speak. In effect, I was awestruck, and can't really describe the extent of the presence to this day. All I know is that I was profoundly moved by the experience.

• You experience strong emotional, physical, or mental reactions, like overwhelming joy, vitality, or peace. I usually experience this when sitting on a beach at sunset. As the pink rays embrace me, I feel happy and tranquil, as if the world is saying hello. This brings me to an important point: Some areas will affect you very powerfully while other people sense nothing whatsoever while in those areas. That's okay. It might be a spot that's sacred to you because you treat it as such.

• You're overwhelmed by the area's beauty or charm, even if it is simple by most standards. If you're not a visual person, this cue might come through other senses. For example, you might become enchanted by a particular creature's song, and it leads you to a spot. You might suddenly feel awakened by a vibrant breeze, or an exquisite aroma might reach out and draw you in.

• You retreated to this place as a child for comfort of thoughtful moments. Alternatively, it is a special place you go to as an adult to gather your thoughts.

I had such a place when I was little. It was a creekside forest where I hid whenever life seemed difficult. No matter what was bothering me, the trees always listened, and the creek kept me "in tune."

• You find natural geometric patterns formed by trees, flowers, grass, stone, flowers, etc. One such place was located on a farmstead in Springville, New York. Just behind the house there was a circle of trees reaching to the heavens. Once beyond that veil of green, everything seemed quiet and calm, and numerous visitors reported fairy sightings in this spot.

• You feel at one with all things and totally at ease with yourself. This is often accompanied with a loss of your time-sense; all time becomes now. For me this happened when I went to Callanish, Scotland. The minute I reached the standing stones, there was no here or there, no yesterday or tomorrow, no self and others. At that moment I truly understood what living presently and in harmony means. Whenever I lose my way, I think back to that experience and it points the way home.

• You regularly receive omens, signs, or direct communications from nature and her citizens. My new backyard is quickly becoming that kind of a power center for me. When we first moved in, I kept finding feathers from different birds: blue, white, and brown. To me, the blue represented happiness, the white, peace, and the brown, solid foundations. Since that day other small gifts from the birds or nature keep appearing with messages for my heart and soul.

If none of these indicators help you discern a power spot, or you're still not certain, one alternative is going on a middle world journey. Ask your totems and guides to show you special spots. Then watch for these places in the real world, or consider if they bear any likenesses to ones already visited.

You can also try dousing to confirm things. The art of dousing was once called water witching because it was a prevalent form of divination for finding well sites. Today, however, many people use dousing to find ley lines and vortexes.

To begin, you'll need one of two things, either a Y-shaped branch or two L-shaped metal rods, the latter of which may be purchased at many New Age stores. Take these to the region in question. If using the branch, take the upper half of the Y, one fork in each hand. If using the rods, hold the shorter end of the L, one rod in each hand.

Next, close your eyes and center yourself on your goal. Breathe deeply. Open your eyes and begin walking. When a source of energy is located, the long end of the Y will start feeling heavy and drawn downward. The long end of the rods will intersect, creating an X (yes, in this case X *does* mark the spot).

Repeat the procedure to confirm the hit. Then continue walking to see what else you find. Hits that appear along a line are likely part of a ley line grid. Hits with one distinct location are probably a power spot, and ones where you get a lot of minor hits that form a circle are probably a vortex.

Once found, decide if you want this to be a private place, or one that you share. Also, please know that it isn't necessary to have such a location for personal practices. You are a power center and sacred space unto yourself. This energy and holiness is a gift of the Creator that goes with you everywhere.

Creating Sacred Space

There are times when you will want to create a sacred space, be it a temporary one for use in ritual, or a permanent one to help heal and strengthen the earth's aura. The process of making temporary sacred space has been covered in many magical and ritual books, so I won't repeat it here. I will say, however, that the real difference between any "normal" room, yard, park, or forest, and one that is sacred really boils down to your attitude. Even a lavatory can be holy if you approach it as such. The urban shaman knows this, and uses this knowledge to help in coping with city living, which doesn't always afford natural, quiet, or overly private locations for worship.

Every culture has had its own way of creating a power center. Some erected standing stones, others blessed the land and gave it suitable offerings, still others held a ritual and declared the area holy. All of these methods are correct, and there are many more of your own devising. What's important here isn't the method, it is the way that you think and act toward that spot. Just as you wouldn't randomly swear or get overly silly in a church, your demeanor when visiting your power center becomes one of veneration, or as Victor Hugo once said: "Whatever be the state of the body, the soul is on its knees."

Beyond this, here are some guidelines to finding the right spot on which to erect a sacred site:

- Bear in mind the ultimate purpose for the site in choosing the area where it will be located. A place where you want to hold tribal rituals, for example, will need to be accessible and comfortable for all your members. An area that you want to use for vision quests needs to be safe and private.

- Bear in mind the major elemental scheme of the area and any key features that might augment your ultimate purpose. For example, areas that might be considered predominantly "water" are better for intuitive efforts because of water's metaphysical nature. Or, an area with a huge old tree might be ideal for trance journeys. An area touched by all four elements is ideal as an "all-purpose" center, or for one that you plan to create specifically to support earth's power grid.

- Bear in mind any cues provided by your guides, totems, and Spirit as to what to look for in your search.

- Bear in mind local laws and attitudes. There are still many cities and towns that don't "hanker" to that "magic stuff," meaning that your efforts won't be received with open arms. Protected or posted tracts of land require permits so you can go there and work. Other places allow hunting, meaning you'll need to take extra precautions in protecting yourself and anyone else creating the site (wear really bright colors).

Once you find the ideal location, the next step is transforming it into holy ground. First, clear away any small bits of brush, rock, or other debris that you might fall over accidentally. Next, give the area a small offering. Perhaps leave some crumbs out for birds, pour out a libation of wine to the soil, plant a special crystal beneath a tree, or whatever. This acts like a letter of introduction to the nature spirits and indicates your desire to work in partnership with them.

Next, decide whether or not you want a designated altar, entryway, exit, directional points, and the like. None of these things is necessary, but they do help establish important markers for your efforts. Additionally, setting up directional points denotes the perimeter of the sacred wheel within which you will be the spoke and the spark of magic.

Once everything is ready, formally dedicate the area in a manner suited to the site, your tradition, and personal vision. Call on your totems and guide to bless the area and visit here with you. Dance and drum to awaken the nature spirits and bid them welcome. Call on the Sacred to fill the entire area with a special radiance, recognizable to anyone with the spiritual eyes to see. Give the spot a name and sing it to the four winds.

Afterward, visit as regularly as possible, bringing small gifts for the land and its creatures, and work your magic here often. Each visit, each spell, each ritual builds power and meaning that will vibrate outward, blessing everyone and everything it touches both now and in the future.

Honoring Sacred Space

Whenever you visit a sacred place, it is very important that you honor the site and the traditions it represents. Not to do so is very insulting to the regional spirits, which can hamper your capacity to ever communicate with them. In all fairness, I will say that there are times when it is hard to know exactly which customs are suitable to a particular site, simply because there's no hands-on information available. But from experience I can tell you that most sites will let you know when you've strayed.

A good example of this happened to me on the Isle of Lewis in Scotland. My husband and I were walking the land, and saw a beautiful heather-covered mound in the distance overlooking the sea. We ventured up to get a better view, but as we touched the mound the birds stopped singing. An audible, unnatural hush fell over the land and we felt chilled to the bone. We were on holy ground, and it wasn't a place we were meant to be. So, Paul and I quickly retreated with a silent apology. After that, everything returned to normal. The land had given its message and we listened. Paying attention to a site's messages is but one way of honoring it. Here are others:

- Approach the area gently and reverently, recognizing its significance, and really taking time to internalize the area's meaning.

- Expect nothing in particular, but hope for everything! If you go in with preconceived notions of what experiences a site might provide, it can easily hinder your receptiveness to other experiences.

- Use the site as it has traditionally been used, if known and possible. For example, when visiting Lourdes, use the water for healing rituals.

- Take nothing from the land other than what's allowed or what nature herself gives you. Remember, we want these wonders preserved for future generations.

- Treat the people of that region and their customs with respect, as you would wish with your own customs. Many of the world's sacred sites were designed by people from different religious paths than ours. Trespassing, rudeness, and other unbecoming conduct provokes ire not only from the residents of that region, but also its spirits.

Finally, since power centers have no particular timetable, and no agenda to fill, they're not going to "perform" at our bidding. So, remain open to nature's spirits and the Sacred, and wait patiently for their input.

Augmenting, Restoring, and Protecting Sacred Space

In your work with sacred places you may periodically run across those that could use an energy boost, restoration, and/or protection. Of these, restoration is the most touchy. While it might be tempting to rush in and start putting things back where you feel they belong, I don't advocate doing so. In fact, I personally believe that, whenever possible, sites should be restored by practitioners of the tradition who built them.

Why? Urban shamanism regards each religious path as being comparable to a specific style of music. Just as a Country Western singer might find it difficult to perform Latin operas perfectly, the practitioners of one magical path cannot necessarily recreate the energy of another tradition's consecrations correctly. What results is a mishmash of energy that doesn't work well together. In effect, you get static.

When it's impossible to get someone from the right tradition to help you restore a site, then perhaps you can get long distance aid and advice over the phone, Internet, or whatever. If you're still having no luck, then at least take the time to research the represented tradition. When no documentation exists about that site or its customs, then you'll have to trust in your inner voice, guides, totems, and the Sacred to help you.

Augmentation and protection, on the other hand, are two things anyone can do. Augmentation amplifies the established vibrations of a power center using tried-and-true methods. These methods support whatever matrix already exists at that site. You can accomplish this through:

- Music—sacred songs, chants, drumming, or spiritual instrumentals move out across the land like a wave of blessing.

223

Take an upper realm journey and find a shaman song just for that site. Or, if you know of a suitable piece of pre-recorded music, play that. For music that keeps on playing even when you're gone, consider hanging up specially chosen wind chimes to ring out magic with every breeze.

- Plants—sow symbolic flowers, trees, herbs, etc., around the region. If you can, make sacred patterns out of them (like a mandala garden). This also fertilizes the earth, carrying your magic into the soil.

- Crystals and Stones—sprinkle tiny charged stones into the soil or running water. Set up miniature megaliths. Add harmonious stones to an altar configuration. Place compatible stones along the ley line or all around the center to illustrate the pattern of power and give it a more refined energy line through which to flow.

- Rituals—the more often rituals occur at a site, the more magic gets absorbed into everything around the area. One of the most potent examples of this I know personally is an area called Dragon Hills, which is a pagan campsite. The land here is filled with quartz to the point where the soil glistens. During each new gathering the vibrations there seem to increase, and even after people leave the land still hums!

- Offerings—small gifts to the land make the nature spirits in that area happy. And a happy spirit makes for better overall energy throughout the region.

- Spiritual visitations—invite your totems and guides to come to this place and grant their special blessings. This brings your augmentation efforts into the astral, making it more multi-dimensional.

Note that whatever you choose should (a) make sense considering the way the site's used, and (b) make sense considering the represented tradition. For example, a site frequently used for weddings would benefit from flowers or crystals that characterize love and commitment, such as roses and pink quartz. Or, a Christian site would be best amplified through traditional Christian music that you find moving.

Now we come to protection. It is a shaman's sacred duty to act as a guardian of the earth's wonders, including power centers and the like. While we might not be able to stand vigil with a sword over such regions, there are some very practical things most of us can do from home or close by.

First, educate others (and yourself). Explain the historical, religious, and spiritual importance of such places to our collective present and future. Second, become politically active. Support individuals who will, in turn, support legislation for site preservation and laws that impose stiff penalties to those who misuse sacred places.

Third, for sites that haven't already been declared a regional or national treasure, circulate petitions so the idea gets before legislators (don't forget to use the Internet as a resource). There are many benefits to this other than safeguarding the site. Many such declarations open the way for grant monies to sustain preservation and restoration efforts.

Fourth, if you have a site nearby, try volunteering some of your time to helping maintain that area. While you are there, you can keep a watchful eye on things, on both material and spiritual levels. If you see something amiss, take care of it.

Finally, since few of us can be forest rangers or tour guides to sacred sites twenty-four hours a day, seven days a week, send out your totem(s) to check on the places you cherish. Create an envelope of positive energy that the creature can carry with it. In shamanism no distance is so great that it cannot be spanned with will and magic.

COMMUNING WITH NATURE

Once a church is built, people go there to commune with God. The shaman uses nature's temples similarly—to commune with the Sacred and the spirits of creation. But this two-way communication is kind of like putting the cart before the horse unless we revisit animistic philosophies, and learn how to integrate them into a very different world than that of our Ancestors.

Animism Today

> *Regard heaven as your father, earth as your mother, and all things as your brothers and sisters.*
> —Oracle of Atsuta

Animism is among one of the earliest forms of religious expression. In ancient times people believed that spirits existed in all things, great and small. Animals, rocks, trees, the wind, insects, the waves—each, and many more, were powerful entities that could be contacted and appeased for a person's or tribe's betterment. For example, a warrior might paint himself or herself with the image of a butterfly to elude the enemy. The butterfly was considered evasive and puzzling; the body painting evoked those attributes in a kind of partial possession or internalization of the butterfly spirit.

As time wore on the veneration of the natural world remained, changing only slightly with regional and cultural transformations. The way in which one honored the spirits became more elaborate, more socialized, but its heart of hearts remained: a deep abiding knowingness that each living thing, and even the universe itself, has a vital essence. This essence is not only a part of creation's tribe, but a power with which to be reckoned.

This animistic worldview is a little difficult for the modern-minded person to comprehend, let alone adapt to. Even I find it hard to regard mosquitoes and roaches as part of my tribe, let alone a spirit to be honored. Nonetheless, if we are to truly awaken and empower the shaman within, we have to get past humano-centric viewpoints. What happens in nature does not revolve around our needs and our wants. If you don't believe me, just ask any survivor of a natural disaster.

I don't necessarily advocate feeling guilty if you step on an ant, or berating yourself each time you use bug spray, but we do have to start thinking and acting differently, one moment at a time. Stop your hurrying long enough to apologize to the ant's spirit, for example…and next time choose a spray that's herbal! With tenacity and practice, animistic attitudes can change our lives and, in turn, benefit the planet tremendously.

Regional and Natural Spirits

Once we accept animism as having merit, the next step is recognizing and communing with various nature spirits. In reading the world's mythology and lore, there is an amazing variety of these creatures whose names, sizes, shapes, and appearances change depending on the culture and setting. Consequently, I'm going to look at things a little generically here, staying true to core shamanism.

Have you ever walked into a house and felt a presence that had a specific demeanor? Trodden down an old wooded path and sensed you weren't alone? Rested beneath the boughs of a great tree and suddenly been aware of its life ebbing beneath and above you? If you answered yes to any of these questions, then you've already had your first tastes of a regional or nature spirit.

Each place and thing has the potential for spirit inhabitation. In manmade objects, the spirit's personality and visage often reflects the object, maker, or inhabitants. In nature, these beings appear similarly to the object to which they're attached, often acting as a guardian. In either case, the spirit of a place gives you access to a lot of good information such as:

- Why an area keeps experiencing a specific type of plant or animal sickness

- How to help the area endure through a drought or other natural disasters

- Where best to put up sacred sites, hold important gatherings, and the like

- What types of plants and animals will thrive here, and what kinds need assistance to stay unendangered

- When it's best to sow, fertilize, and harvest various plants

There are two common ways in which you can meet a regional or location spirit, the first being through trance journeys, as covered earlier in this book. The second is through a simple meditation. Sit and breathe deeply, facing the direction in which you feel the spirit resides. Allow your vision to blur; look at nothing in particular. As you watch, a face or symbol might begin to materialize in a rock, a hill, or whatever. This is the spirit saying "hello."

At this point you may ask questions of the spirit, but keep it pertinent and respectful. Location and regional spirits can help in healing entire communities if asked the right questions with the right intention. Don't, for example, ask a mountain spirit how to solve a problem in the valley—it may not know that. Also, try to keep the conversation short. Spirits have other duties to attend to than talking to us.

During your discourse, some very large regional spirits can sometimes feel a bit overwhelming. The mountain spirit, for example, might wrap itself around you, or a cloud spirit might loom high and huge overhead. Don't let this imagery frighten you. It's simply an astral projection of that entity's power and importance to the region.

At some point in the meditation you'll notice your ability to concentrate waning or the clarity of communication diminishing. This is a good sign that it's time to stop. Thank the spirit for its aid, and ask if it has a name by which you can call on it again. Then return to normal levels of awareness with a thankful heart for the knowledge you received.

HEALING THE WORLD TREE

We all share the same earth Mother, regardless of race or country of origin, so let us learn the ways of love, peace, and harmony, and seek the good paths in life.

—Sun Bear

Urban shamans recognize that the world will not recover from all human abuses overnight. Nor can this happen without real effort on both physical and spiritual levels. Unfortunately for the better part of the twentieth century, the spiritual dimension has been overlooked. Shamans can help fill that gap by traveling the world tree, bearing healthful waters, healing salve, and rose petals of love with them.

Begin your journey in the lower realm, asking your guides and totems to join you. Feed the roots of the great tree with water, seeing it as rainbow-colored light. Continue pouring the water until the ground can absorb no more, then move yourself to the middle realm.

At the middle realm leave an offering of some sort for the nature spirits. Apologize to them for any known or unknown wrongdoing on your part, so the lines of communication remain open. Then, look around at the tree's branches and bark. Apply your magical salve to any open wounds liberally, again visualizing it as filled with light, and absorbing effortlessly into the wood.

Last of all, travel to the upper realm. Cast the rose petals on the fray, dispersing the energy of your love and compassion for the earth. Then stop and wait quietly. Let your spiritual ears seek out a special healing song for the Mother. This is the song you will take back with you to real time, one that you can ring out loud and strong—a song that can sing the world into wholeness along with your soul.

applied urban shamanism

To grasp god in all things—this is the sign
of your new birth.

—Meister Eckhart

In Chapter 1, I mentioned that a shaman walks between worlds, maintaining a delicate balance between Spirit and today's reality. Nowhere is this balancing act more difficult or challenging than in the city, among hundreds of people who neatly compartmentalize the Sacred away from everyday life. It is one thing to use shamanic techniques, and another altogether to function adequately as a shaman in this setting.

Life's pace makes it seem like we live in the middle of a whirlwind where it's hard to breathe sometimes, let alone get a glimpse of the Sacred. Our work schedules go on; family responsibilities go on; social obligations go on. Be that as it may, we can't turn back the clock and live in simpler, less technically sophisticated times. Nor can we insulate ourselves and our tribes from outside influences that could potentially detract or derail tradition and spirituality. If anything, in the quest to live presently, the urban shaman dives wholeheartedly into the fray of modern life, to help draw the Sacred back into our world on a global level.

So, the urban shaman's calling isn't necessarily easy—most worthwhile things aren't. Instead of feeling discouraged by the challenge, however, we can hold tightly to shamanic philosophies as a support system, and keep on "keepin' on" in a manner befitting the Ancestors. Why keep going? Because we know that the application of shamanic principles is something that could really help us and others to live harmoniously and joyfully in the concrete jungle.

Urban shamanism is more than a philosophy and more than a religion. It gives people a way to keep in touch with Mother and Spirit, to rediscover the Higher Self and a meaningful inner mythology, and to find wholeness while healing others and the earth. It also helps us repattern the way we think and live so we get beyond the dogma, begin trusting in our dreams, and start transforming our daily lives into something more "alive" and fulfilling.

One great helpmate to being an effective urban shaman is having the right tools for the job. Every religious tradition has specific tools designed to help practitioners focus on something other than the 9 A.M. to 5 P.M. world. Urban shamans are no different, but perhaps a little more inventive. You'll want to create a shamanic "kit" of sorts by blending tradition, earth-friendly outlooks, ingenuity, and modern realities together into a functional system, including the way in which your tools are found or made.

TOOLS OF THE TRADE

> *Each is given a bag of tools, a shapeless mass, a*
> *book of rules; And each must make, ere life is*
> *flown, a stumbling block or a stepping stone.*
> —R. L. Sharpe

In earlier chapters, I have discussed the intuitive process that goes with choosing, finding, or making your tools. The purpose of this

231

section is to round out those processes with ideas and/or hands-on instructions for making or finding those tools with a unique, urban shaman's flair.

Costume

The purpose of a costume is honoring a spirit or creating an alternate persona for ritual purposes. You can certainly make or rent appropriate costumes for your purposes if time and money allow. But what's neat about the urban shaman's garb is that even a business suit can become a costume if you look at it with a creative eye. Nearly everything we wear carries specific meaning and symbolism for us, depending on when we wear it and how those clothes make us feel. The trick is in using that symbolism effectively.

For example, if you don't have time to make a costume that portrays winter's spirit for a seasonal observance, you could use a winter coat, hat, mittens, and boots instead. Come spring, dress similarly, but ritually remove the warm regalia as a symbolic way to welcome the warm wind spirits. For a summer ritual, use a bathing suit as an appropriate costume to honor the sun spirit, and in fall, wear something with a harvest print to please the plant spirits who have given you such abundance.

Want to connect with a tree spirit? How about covering a hat with fall leaves or making a piece of clothing out of recycled paper? Commune with a flower spirit? Wear a floral shirt and don some perfume made from that flower. Hold a rite of passage ritual? Consider having the youth begin by wearing a makeshift cloth diaper, then change sometime during the ritual into adult clothing. All these ideas, and similar ones of your own devising, are practical ways to bring the shamanic art of costuming back into our twentieth century world.

Crystals, Stones, Minerals

The earth is very generous in her gifts to us, and thanks to New Age marketing, stones and minerals are readily available to urban shamans through mail order catalogues, New Age stores, science shops, and the like. One source in particular that I'm comfortable in recommending is Blue Pearl/Lotus Light (phone 1-800-822-4810 for a catalogue). If these sources seem to lack what you're looking for, try calling the geology department of a college or a science museum for information, or going to rock shows and pagan gatherings as they come to your area.

I feel that a lot of commercial sources for stones are overpriced. So, whenever you can, walk the land and let earth provide. I am constantly amazed at what kinds of rocks I find even in the city—like dark black flint, which is a wonderful grounding stone. Then too, some manmade stones also have potential if we look at them with a discerning eye. For example, a bit of brick can represent building a safe haven, concrete can symbolize firm foundations, and a bit of blacktop depicts the way to "pave" a path to a particular goal.

If you are unfamiliar with the metaphysical associations for stones, crystals, and minerals, here's a brief list of the more readily available ones for your reference:

STONE, MINERAL, AND CRYSTAL CORRESPONDENCES

Agate	Agate's attributes change according to its colors and patterning. Green agate is often favored among urban shamans for its ability to improve a garden's productivity. An eye agate (dark with concentric white circles) is excellent for protection, and predominantly white agate improves truthfulness.
Amber	Best purchased in beads for the budget-minded shaman, amber is a fire stone that connects us with Father Sky and the sun. Wearing amber strengthens your magical power.
Amethyst	A dreaming stone that calms, soothes, and generally

helps the bearer live more presently with less stress. Amethyst also reintegrates the psychic self with everyday awareness.

Beryl   A good stone to carry or wear when trying to communicate with weather spirits. Beryl also grants vision and allays fear.

Bloodstone   A stone that fosters healing, including emotional healing.

Brass   This metal draws prosperity and helps protect any item that you value when placed nearby.

Carnelian   This stone improves self-confidence, especially for public speaking. It is also a helpmate to successful trance journeys.

Cat's eye   This strengthens the conscious mind and acts to improve financial situations.

Citrine   An excellent addition to dream catchers, as this allays nightmares.

Copper   A wonderful choice for directing energy where you want it to go, especially in healing.

Coral   This gift of the waters confers inner peace and thoughtfulness.

Flint   The spirit of this stone helps the shaman in healing rituals. It also protects against mischievous nature spirits.

Hematite   Use this to ground and center yourself, and live presently.

Iron   An anti-magic metal, iron also protects against spirits whose natures have been warped somehow.

Jasper   Hold this to commune with the rain spirits and encourage luck.

Lapis   The lapis spirit brings us closer to sacred powers by increasing our devotion and opening spiritual pathways.

Lava	This gift from deep within Earth Mother's womb protects the bearer. When wrapped in a leaf and placed back into the earth, it grants healing.
Lead	Keeping this near your doorway will safeguard your home and the residents from harm and negative magic.
Lodestone	Use this to attract the energies you most need and to improve your will.
Moonstone	A good choice for inspiring self-love and improving overall hopefulness.
Pumice	Available sometimes in soap, pumice banishes problems and negativity.
Salt	A wonderful mineral for cleansing, safety, and keeping both feet on the ground.
Silver	Helps invoke spirits, improves psychic impressions, and encourages integration of spiritual concepts.
Sodalite	This stone calms one's spirit. Try holding it while you pray or meditate.
Steel	Add this to dream catchers to keep away bad dreams.
Tin	Put this in power pouches for luck.
Turquoise	Turquoise protects during travel, including through the astral landscape.

Drum

Nearly anything can become a drum. If you don't believe me, just watch children some time, or the wonderful percussion group Stomp. Both can take chopsticks and any surface and begin drumming! Old coffee and potato chip containers transform into drums simply by putting the plastic top back on. Or, perhaps try using tight-fitting fabrics over the opening to see what kind of sounds you can get.

Close up a cardboard box and rap on it (the larger the size, the lower the tone and louder the sound). Put different-sized glasses upside down and tap them with a knife for high pitches. Do likewise with kitchen pots and pans using a wooden spoon as a striker. Wooden bowls, mixing bowls, and other sturdy dinnerware work equally well. The key here is finding something handy that has a sound that you like, and then let your inner shaman take over.

Dream Catcher

In Chapter 6, I reviewed the importance of dreams to the shaman's worldview. As such, a dream catcher is an important tool. Unfortunately, many of those available on the market are overpriced. So what's the urban shaman on a budget to do but make one herself or himself (this is also a good project for kids—see Chapter 7).

Begin by finding any circular base, preferably a natural one like rose branches fashioned into a circle, a thin circle of wood, tightly bound herbs braided into a wreath, or anything similar. While most Native Americans use sinue for the netting on a dream catcher, you can turn to wool or cotton yarn, heavy twine or string, or variegated ribbons. Also gather together some feathers, beads, crystals, dried herbs, silk flowers, charms, and the like in case you want to add them into the design. Some of the items known to inspire peaceful sleep, psychic dreams, or ward off nightmares include:

Amethyst	Basil	Jasmine	Rosemary
Azurite	Lotus	Marigold	Lavender
Silver	Morning glory	Rose	Chamomile
Quartz	Anise	Cedar	Mint

Note that if you can't find a listed flower or herb, you can use an aromatic oil instead. In this case simply dab it around the edge, moving clockwise as you go to inspire positive energy.

There's no right or wrong way to create the net. Let your inner voice and the Ancestors guide you, keeping in mind the tool's function while you work. I do suggest, however, regularly putting small knots in the design so it doesn't easily loosen up or pull apart. When you're done, pray over the catcher, bless it, and hang it over your bed.

By the way, this design works very well for other purposes than inspiring dreams. For example, make one with protective tokens attached to it and put it on the front door to filter out negativity. Make another one with good luck charms on it and hang it off the rearview mirror of a car, and another still for success and keep it near your computer.

Fire Sources

With so many people living in apartments these days, having usable fire sources isn't as easy as it once was. Many small homes and most apartments don't have a fireplace, and others have regulations governing fire sources for insurance reasons. Some dwelling facilities require self-contained candles, for example.

I found this issue frustrates many urban shamans because they *want* to gather around a tribal fire of some sort. My solution is a symbolic one. Gather around a heating vent, the kitchen stove (or microwave), or around a central lighting fixture (portable book lamps work well, as do glow sticks). All these things are contemporary equivalents of fire.

You might want to decorate the vent, stove, or lighting fixture somehow so that it has a special appeal for that ritual. Or, hang dried herbs over the vent, boil potpourri on the stove, and dab essential oil on the lamp so that each gives off an aroma suited to the occasion.

Herbs

Herbal arts crop up again and again in shamanic traditions for everything from healing to blessing. Thanks to having supermarkets nearby, we all have a pretty good selection of herbs available to us at all times. For more unusual items, try food cooperatives, import shops, and international markets.

In choosing which herbs to incorporate into your urban kit, look first to those that you use regularly at home. No one ever said you had to give up economy for spiritual pursuits. Next, consider if you have a means to keep fresh herbs for a while; fresh herbs are considered more potent magically. Some, such as rosemary, freeze exceptionally well, preserving the energy. Just make sure both your fresh and dried herbs are free of molds and any debris that could hinder both flavor and spiritual effectiveness.

At home, make sure you label everything (inside and out) clearly. One leafy or powdered herb can look a lot like another, and if you're using them for cooking magic, a mix-up might not be edible (or safe). Also try to keep your herbs away from heat and light, both of which drain energy and flavor.

When local sources fail to provide you with the herbs you need, here are two mail order suppliers that I use frequently:

Lotus Light Products
Box 2
Wilmot, WI 53192
800-824-6396

Frontier Herbs
3021 78th St., Box 299
Norway, IA 53218
800-669-3275

Both suppliers have excellent prices, offer organics, and provide prompt shipping.

Incense and Aromatics

Some of the traditional aromatics, and the ritual uses of incense are covered in Chapter 2, such as the use of sage for vision quests, communing with the Ancestors, or spirit travel, and cedar or sweetgrass for purifying smudge sticks. There are certainly plenty of commercial aromatics and incenses available, but some may contain chemical additives or synthetic fragrances. Chemicals and synthetics make an aromatic or incense magically void, so you may want to make some for yourself.

Any very dry herbs, citrus rind, flower petals, etc., that are finely ground may be burned as incense if you have a fire-safe container. One easy option is purchasing some self-lighting charcoal and putting it in a bed of sand or dirt. Set the container on a trivet to protect sensitive surfaces from heat. Light the charcoal and wait until it's hot, then sprinkle in the chosen herb a little at a time until you get the amount of smoke (and aroma) desired. Using this method, it is pretty easy to mix and blend three to four symbolically significant herbs as long as you remember that they don't always smell the same when burning as they do dry or fresh.

A second good method is similar to the one above except that you begin with about a cup of ground wood shavings. I use an old pencil sharpener to grind up the kind of wood I want. I also sweep up my husband's carpentry scraps, and ask friends to gather any shavings when cutting wood for home fireplaces.

Pine burns very well and has a nice base scent for almost any blend. Oak is a good choice for a long-burning incense with a neutral base scent. If you're looking for a particular type of wood for symbolic purposes, check a good lumber supply shop, carpentry centers, or a craft store. These places are likely to stock more exotic woods.

Add dried aromatics to this, one tablespoonful at a time, and test the resulting blend on a fire source. Some people use an old blender to mix the dry ingredients so they get well-incorporated. I also sometimes sift the dry compound to get out big chunks—this helps the mixture burn more evenly.

Alternatively, you can mix aromatic oils to the ground wood. I suggest adding oils into the base two to three drops at a time, stirring regularly and checking the scent, so that the blend doesn't get too pungent. Afterward, let the blend dry before storing it so it doesn't get moldy, and sift it as before for an even consistency.

With either of these methods or a mixture of the two, you can always adjust the final formula to make it more pleasing. If you find your incense's aroma is overwhelming when burned, simply add more wood power to dilute it, and test it again. If it's too weak, add more aromatics.

Store the finished incense in a dry, dark area, preferably in an airtight container. From my experience I'd say the incense retains a good aroma for about six to eight months, so make only what you can use in that time span. To extend the longevity of the blend, add a teaspoon of benzoin powder as a fixative.

Masks

Traditionally, people made masks out of a variety of natural materials, including metal, stone, wood, clay, basketry weaving, corn husks, and papier mâché. Decorations on the surface were just as diversified, including rope fiber, fur, teeth, beans, grain, shells, bark, feathers, hair, leaves, soil, sand, stones, and other suitable components, considering the goal at hand. To this list, the urban shaman can add hundreds of other handy household items, including:

magic markers	scrap fabric	cardboard
wrapping paper	greeting cards	magazine pictures
paint	ribbons	buttons
crayons	cork	powdered herbs
silk flowers	nuts and bolts	computer parts (used)
glitter	construction paper	candle wax
stickers	noodles	matches (representing fire)
broom clippings	coupons	bottle caps

Here are just a few examples of how you can put these mask materials together:

- In making a mask to appease technological spirits or to improve your memory, use a piece of an old memory chip from the computer over the third-eye portion of the mask. Decorate the rest of the mask with symbols suited to your goal, or with other symbolic components.

- In making a spring mask to welcome the sun, color the base gold or red, add some golden glitter, and then glue matches around the entire perimeter of the mask, match heads facing outward. The final effect looks like a sun in splendor.

- In making a mask for a ritual or spell to draw more affection into your life, cut out the messages or signatures from a bunch of old greeting cards. These already have the positive energy that comes from others' good wishes and feelings toward you, so they will harmonize with your goal.

- In making a mask to honor and commune with your cat familiar, use a few broom clippings for the whiskers, and fur gathered from brushing the cat as part of the base. Sprinkle a little catnip into the blend to improve rapport.

As you can see, you need not have fancy components to make really meaningful, fun masks for your rituals. All you really need is a good imagination!

Medicine Bundles

Traditionally, a medicine bundle is a small cache of treasured power objects gathered from nature, but the urban shaman might choose to include potent symbolic tokens from the human domain as well. Each token is one that has some intense personal shamanic experience attached to it—something that distinguishes that object and its energy as special.

Despite the name, this bundle may actually be constructed from a swatch of cloth or fur, a pouch, a wooden or glass box, or possibly a purse. Whatever the housing, I strongly suggest it be durable to protect your treasures, and portable so you can take it with you easily. Even Food storage containers works, but I suggest wrapping the contents in natural fabric to avoid touching the plastic and to maintain their integrity.

Your medicine bundle is not something that has a maximum or minimum number of objects. You can add and take away things as Spirit moves you. For example, if you had a particularly strong feeling of safety that led to acquiring a small stone, and suddenly felt the need for protection, you might take out the stone and plant it in the ground near your living space.

About the only real restriction that goes with medicine bundles is that most shamans consider this a highly personal object, not something for show-and-tell. Many of the tokens within will be used in trance journeys to rekindle a specific energy; others will emanate their power for you every day. So this is something to care for and cherish, not to display randomly.

It is possible to make medicine or power bundles for specific purposes by gathering objects that symbolize that purpose, blessing them, and putting them in a suitable container. It is also possible to make bundles for other people. When doing so, you should include something personal from that individual so it complements the recipient's energy.

Medicine Shields

As a brief reminder of its significance, in completed form your medicine shield will be a physical representation of your life essence, chosen path, acquired knowledge, a vision of wholeness, and your sense of connection to the universe. To this spiritual foundation other specifics may be added to represent what you most need, but I highly recommend making one basic shield first that's all-purpose.

You can begin with a base of stiffened cloth, canvas, cardboard, wood, leather, or even plain heavy paper. Singular-purpose shields can be as small or as large as you like. I suggest, however, that your main one be big enough to become a prominent centerpiece to your rituals (these shields make a good meditative focus, too).

Leather and other absorbent bases take well to aromatic oils. Adding these will give the shield broader sensual appeal. Rub the chosen oil evenly into the surface *before* coloring it, as the oil can change the hues of the dyes/paints slightly. Let the surface dry before proceeding with painting.

Consider making the stains, dyes, or paints for coloring the shield out of natural items like berries, roots, and barks. If possible, choose plants that also have symbolic value. Many nice colors can be extracted fairly easily by steeping the plant matter in warm vinegar. This coloring will likely fade with time, though, so you may want to add fixatives like alum mixed with cream of tartar. If you decide to use commercial colorings instead, please find something nontoxic. Toxicity detracts from the "healthy" aspect of the shield.

Gather together any symbolic items you want to adhere to the shield. Tree sap makes a good alternative to conventional glue. Or take any liquid glue and mingle finely powdered herbs with it so that the final adhesive appeals to your higher senses. Once you have everything you want for construction, return to the instructions in Chapter 3 on the process for approaching the shield's decoration, and start to work.

Noisemakers and Rattles

Noisemakers and rattles serve numerous functions in shamanism. They announce one's presence to nature spirits, call the Ancestors, invoke various types of weather (usually rain), and ward off evil influences. Percussion also accompanies the shaman's song, helps the shaman achieve altered states of awareness, and acts as an alternative drum. Much to our benefit, the urban shaman has plenty of options available for making this essential tool from regular household items. For example:

- Take an empty paper towel roll, fill it with beans, popcorn, rice, or other small, dry items, and then cap the ends with foil or cloth. This becomes a makeshift rain stick.

- You can create a version of clicksticks from two wooden chopsticks gathered from any Chinese restaurant, or for that matter, two fallen branches. Another alternative is using two pieces of silverware (note the playing of spoons as an instrument in some Country music).

- Food storage containers with buttons, coins, macaroni, or tiny pebbles inside sound really neat, and if you add a little yogurt or water to this mixture, the sound blends into a "swish-thud."

- The same coffee can you used for a drum can be filled with various small items to turn it into a rattle. Glass jars with corks or canning jars also work well.

Any coverable object that has a hollow area can become a functional noisemaker. And come fall, don't forget nature's rattle, the ever-handy gourd! Just let it dry, and it will work as a rattle nearly forever.

Offerings

Throughout this book I've talked about bringing small offerings with you for nature's spirits, so having a variety of suitable offerings in your shaman's kit might not be a bad idea. In the past, people commonly gave of their food, fabrics, beverages, coins, and anything they truly valued to show their respect and appreciation. The urban shaman seeks to do so similarly, but keeps in mind the planet's welfare in his or her choices. Additionally, we have a lot more offerings to choose from.

In looking around your personal space for potential offerings, bear in mind the following:

- The item should be something you value, or something deeply meaningful to you, as were the offerings the Ancients gave (see Chapter 2, the section on "Key Components of Ritual").

• The item should have some symbolic meaning, either to your spell/ritual or to the spirits being propitiated. For example, if working a ritual for prosperity, you might "give away" some change you've saved to a good cause, so that you're open to receive the universe's blessings.

• The item should also have practical value whenever possible. For example, a good offering for an earth-healing ritual would be homemade compost given to the earth. To add more meaning to the blend, make it during a harvest moon to symbolize a flourishing earth.

• The item should be natural (e.g., biodegradable) if it will be left outside.

• The item should make sense, considering the type of offering you're giving. For example, burnt offerings need to be readily flammable—don't use green wood, beverages, etc., in this setting.

• The item should be portable if you're taking it to a special location, and of a suitable size considering the area in which you're planning to leave it. For example, if taking an offering to a nearby park, you'll probably want to keep it small enough that you can hide it from people who might accidentally disturb the gift.

Remember, too, that not all offerings have to be left where you're holding a ritual, casting a spell, or going on a trance journey. Actions like sharing what you have with someone in need, or taking personal time to help others, are both types of offerings that rejoice the spirits, the Ancestors, and the Sacred.

Portable Altars

The entire earth can be an altar from which the shaman gathers sacred tools, but there are times when we want something a little more formal. However, in a transitory and sometimes intolerant society, it is not always practical to have a huge, hardwood table display. When you're faced with this kind of difficulty, the portable altar is a perfect solution.

Portable altars are a little like shaman's spheres (see Chapter 7). In this case, you'll be starting with a clear, two-sided ball. These can often be found in craft shops from late October until December, for making ornaments. Take one-half of the ball and fill it with gifts from the earth and sacred objects. Gather things like the ashes from a ritual fire, a fallen feather, a stone from a pond or creek, a pine clipping from near your home, a lucky penny, etc.

Put these objects inside the sphere and seal it, thereby sealing the spell and the magic within. Hang this off your car's rearview mirror. If you don't have a car, use a smaller plastic sphere and then carry it in a purse, suitcase, briefcase, or whatever. For closets or rooms, poke holes in the upper half of the sphere with a hot nail, and make sure to add some nice aromatics to the blend within.

As a side note, these can make quite lovely ornaments and gifts during the holiday season.

Prayers

I've included prayers as part of your shaman's kit because they're something you can carry in your heart and use anywhere, any time. Be that as it may, you'd be surprised at how many people have no idea how to pray, or how to create personal or group prayers. Our society has gotten away from having the Sacred as its nucleus, and thus the intimacy of prayers has suffered. Many individuals have retreated to a safe distance, using rote prayers whose words they don't even think about. This is not what the shaman's prayers should be.

A shaman's prayer begins with thoughtfulness and trust. Thoughtfulness helps us to pray about what we most need, instead of just what we might "want." Trust helps us release the energy of our prayers into the hands of higher powers. If we don't believe in the Sacred's and Ancestors' ability to help us, then prayer is a just waste of energy.

Shamans often use prayers passed down through tradition, but will often alter these slightly to be more personal and comfortable. Few people these days find that King James-type prayers flow effortlessly from their tongues. So, prayer, while it might begin in a standard form, ends at the heart with meaningful words that really express individuality.

A shaman prays diligently and sincerely, knowing that sometimes one must wait on the Sacred for an answer. Thus we come to the next step in prayer—silence and waiting. Give the Ancestors and the Sacred time to respond and speak directly to your heart.

After you pray, don't forget to follow up mundanely by doing everything possible to make your prayers a reality. Shamans recognize that ours is a partnership with Spirit. So while an expectant, thankful heart does much to help manifest prayer, two willing hands and old-fashioned hard work certainly doesn't hurt!

Talking Stick

I have seen some of the most interesting, unique, creative, and beautiful talking sticks in my travels. The most interesting was made from an old copper pipe that a person found in the cellar. She cleaned it up, added some braided silver wire, feathers, and metal etching, and then started using it. When I inquired as to the reasons behind this particular choice, the creator replied that anything that conducted water could also "conduct" spirit effectively!

The most unique and creative talking stick I've seen was made by a young child who devised hers from the inner tube of a paper towel roll. She colored it, glued on very tiny stones, and stuffed some scrap cloth inside so it would be a little sturdier. When I asked her why she chose this medium, she said it honored the earth by recycling. Out of the mouths of babes…

With these two examples in mind, any long-handled item can be turned into a talking stick. I still favor using fallen branches, but urban shamans sometimes need fast, simple alternatives. Try a broom handle, a candle (wrap this so it doesn't get soft when handled), a wooden spoon (a great choice for "kitchen witches"), an old antenna (great for directing energy), and the like.

If you can find a fallen branch and want to work with it, you'll probably want to soak or sand off the bark first. This will make it easier to burn designs into the wood and to set in crystals. For setting the crystals and getting off particularly stubborn parts of the bark, get a set of wood awls at a craft shop or hardware store. Just be careful, because these tools are very sharp. When you're first working with carving tools, it's easy to push too hard and get cut.

Set your stones using a mixture of reliable glue and herbs to help offset any chemical additives in the glue. Add a hand-hold of some sort if you wish. I sometimes use thick fabric trim or scrap leather attached by ribbon or thong for this purpose. This gives me a handy place from which to hang feathers, power bundles, satchels of incense, and other shamanic kit components.

When the stick is completed, oil the wood regularly to keep it from drying out. I usually suggest lemon oil, but a walnut oil scented with a symbolic aromatic is a nice alternative.

Totemic Representations

Most shamans like to have handy representations of the creatures who protect, guide, and teach us in our path. Thankfully, the New Age movement has inspired many gift shops to carry stone carvings, garden statuary, jewelry pieces, picture frames, pewter and crystal figurines, brass and wood forms, candles, posters, children's toys, and even cakes that depict our animal companions. In the latter instance, you are what you eat!

When your budget won't allow you to buy one of these, the urban shaman isn't lost. Try looking through greeting cards, old magazines, calendars, pet food boxes (and sometimes human food boxes too—note Tony the Tiger), used books, newspapers, postage stamps, advertising mailers (i.e., coupons), scrap fabrics, and kids' coloring books. For example, when I was searching for a fish image (my main element is water), I found a nice shark portrayed on the wrapping of my computer paper. This might be used to represent a fiercely protective water spirit.

Once you find a suitable image, meditate with it, take it with you on your trance journeys, and keep it in a place of honor. Remember, it doesn't matter if it's made from plastic or gold as long as you treasure what it represents.

SPELL AND RITUAL COMPONENTS

> *A ceremonial object isn't necessary for worship,*
> *but it certainly makes it more fun.*
>
> —Scout Cloud Lee

Once our tools are made or gathered, the next step is having a handy set of components for spellcraft and ritual work. The urban shaman has a wealth of options available to him or her. For example, when you don't have quartz handy for healing or vision work, how about your watch? Digital watches are usually powered by quartz crystals. Or, if you don't have a feather to transport you to the spirit realm, how about one from a pillow or feather duster?

Here are two more good examples: Some native shamans sometimes use yellow pollen in spells aimed at keeping a person from getting lost. We might translate this into carrying a dandelion from our lawn so that we always return home safely. Another tradition is that of carrying white corn for providence and abundance. Why not use white popcorn instead?

To be honest, I can't think of anything in my house that couldn't potentially be used in urban shamanism as a spell or ritual focus (see the section on "Urban Symbolism" later in this chapter). Obviously, the more natural an item is the better, but when you're surrounded by anything *but* nature, use what's handy! Take a ballpoint pen in hand for directing energy into communication issues, a glue stick to "hold things together," a mirror to reflect negativity, inside-out clothing to "turn" luck around, and so forth. The trick here is simply thinking differently and being able to see the potential magic in even the most mundane of things.

TIMING IS EVERYTHING...OR IS IT?

> *Life can be clearer and easier when we just give*
> *in and say "yes."*
>
> —Debra Farrington

There are several schools of magic that rely heavily on timing as being important to any procedure's effectiveness. The urban shaman, however, is often faced with schedules and circumstances that don't allow for 2 A.M. rituals beneath a full moon, or similar constraining requisites. So when a traditional observance takes place at dawn and you just can't make it, what happens? Does all your effort get lost because of a few hours difference? I don't think so.

Urban shamans have a very pragmatic outlook on life that sometimes requires "winging it." If you can't be up at 2 A.M., how about earlier in the evening beneath a street lamp? If you can't be out of the house at dawn because you're getting ready for work, how about going earlier and taking a symbolic light source with you like a flashlight, and turning it on during your effort?

There are absolutely no limits to how inventive you can get as long as the end result is something meaningful and real. If you have problems adjusting to this type of thinking, just remember that time is a human construct, not a spiritual one. No matter where you are, it's 2 A.M. somewhere in the world. The Ancestors and the Sacred live outside of time, and magic travels outside of time, so there's no reason to be bound by it unless we so choose.

URBAN SYMBOLISM

All that is visible must grow beyond itself.

Symbolism is very important to shamanism, and to all magical traditions. Symbols are used in meditation, talisman creation, fetish construction, potion blending, power center blessings, and absolutely every mystical procedure I've ever read about. But yesterday's symbols don't always match today's reality. For example, in old dream dictionaries from the 1900s, gloves are listed as an emblem of propriety. Now we might consider them symbolic of a picky personality (the white glove test) or gentle handling (kid gloves).

Societal, cultural, technological, and personal changes are happening nearly as quickly as I change my socks. Consequently, I believe that the urban shaman has to alter or adapt traditional imagery to better fit the world's transformations. This way his or her symbols always remain fresh, meaningful, and vital, rather than impersonal and stagnant.

Yes, there are some representations that have timeless appeal. The cross, for example, will always symbolize Christianity, the four elements, and the cardinal points. But, there are hundreds of new potential symbols emerging around us every day. The computer is a good example, representing the gathering of knowledge, among other things. Here's a list of just a few others that will hopefully inspire ideas of your own:

URBAN SYMBOLISM

Airplane	The air element, rising above circumstances, perspectives, movement, travel
Blender	Integrating information, blending diverse things into harmony
Calculator	Logic, forethought, attentive living

Computer disks	Gathering information, retrieving skills or knowledge from the subconscious
Crockpot	Slow but steady progress, especially emotional
Disposal	Getting rid of the literal and figurative garbage in your life
Electrical outlet	Reconnection, power, directing energy
Freezer	Cooling heated tempers, halting negativity
Internet	Networking, communication, expanding awareness, life's web, recognizing our magical tribe
Laptop computer	Taking the magic with you, accessibility
Lawn mower	Clearing away old or outmoded thoughts and ways of living, evening things out
Microscope	Looking closely at life or situations and seeing them clearly; realness
Paperclip/stapler	Holding things together, connection
Remote	The power to make and change our reality. Initiate!
Satellite dish	Seeking out the truth and receiving it when discovered
Skyscraper	Reaching a goal, realizing ambitions, upward movement
Synthesizer	Magical mimicry
Telephone	Communication, messages, rapport
Telescope	Turning one's attention outward to new possibilities and potentials
VCR	The ability to review a situation or circumstances thoughtfully

As a functional illustration, say you want to improve your financial flow. How about taking a green or gold piece of paper and inscribing a dollar sign on it. Then fold this into an airplane, focus on your intention, and fly it on the winds to give the spell some motion! In another example, if you're not very good at imitation, how about using a synthesizer to mimic your totem to welcome it in the sacred space?

Again, the medium isn't the issue of what makes for good magic, it's the meaning. The more emotional, sensual, and spiritual significance your symbols have to whatever procedure you're embarking on, the more powerful, transformational, and enduring the results will be.

PARTING THOUGHTS

During the writing of this book I had some observations, thoughts, and insights about shamanism that I'd like to share with you before closing:

- I believe that anyone can integrate shamanic ideals and methods into his or her tradition. Shamanism has a very broad worldview, and an even broader view of the universal powers. Consequently, much of its philosophy works very well in any setting in which you find yourself, and any path on which you walk.

- Core shamanism has many advantages and one central drawback. It does not focus on any one tribal heritage. Consequently, you'll often feel like a square peg in a round hole when working with a traditional shaman who has a culture and ancestry behind him or her. Additionally, that shaman may not consider your "way" as anything that vaguely resembles shamanism, because of the cultural influence. Please bear this in mind as you practice, and do your best to honor all shamanic paths as part of the great circle.

- All shamanic traditions had specific names for the various spirits worshipped in nature. The spirit's name was often quite simple and reflective of its purpose or place, such as "water woman." While I could not list the expanse of shamanic entities in a format such as this, you may want to look into them further so that you can call on traditional spirits that mirror your path and goal(s). Three books suited to researching shamanic spirits and deities are: *Guide to the Gods*, by Marjorie Leach (ABC Clio, 1992), *Encyclopedia of Gods*, by Michael Jordan (Facts on File, 1993), and *Goddesses in World Mythology*, by Martha Ann and Dorothy Imel (Oxford University Press, 1993).

• Similarly, all tribal/shamanic settings had a specific wheel of the year that they followed as a microcosm of the great circle. Within this wheel, other rituals and observances of a more personal nature took place. Should you decide to embark on a particular culturally centered shamanic path, it would be well worth your time to study these celebrations and find ways to integrate them into daily life.

Last, but perhaps most importantly, while one may use shamanic methods and ideals, that doesn't automatically make you a shaman, a medicine man, or a medicine woman. These are honorable titles, given by Spirit or a tribe, as someone earns them. We need to take care in how we use such designations in our communities so as not to do a disservice to those who do, indeed, deserve the station and recognition.

LIVING THE PATH

Like all shamans, the urban shaman seeks aliveness. He or she seeks to be fully present and real in life, as an active participant in it, and as a co-creator with the Divine. Once awakened to the full potential of the shaman within ourselves, we too can begin to live those beliefs every moment of every day. This lifestyle creates cohesion and a constant flow of positive energy. It also weaves the Sacred, the Ancestors, and Spirits back into everything possible, so that our entire reality expresses faith, and is alive with magic.

Let it begin today.

afterWORD

A rather interesting thing happened to me while writing this book, something that I felt you might enjoy reading about. Several years ago I bought myself a beautiful dream catcher decorated with a lovely brown and white mottled feather. At some point my loving cats in good-intentioned humor decided to steal the feather. It disappeared into their treasure trove without a trace…until now.

Just as mysteriously as that feather wafted into a black hole, it reappeared on top of my computer when I was halfway through writing *Shaman in a 9 to 5 World!* I took it as a good sign from Spirit not only for this book, but for my personal life and path as well. Things had been rather rough…we were in the middle of moving, our truck died, and the entire house was in chaos. Yet in the midst of that disarray, the feather floated gently down to bless this text and bring a smile to my face.

Anyone who thinks Spirit lacks in humor, doesn't know Spirit.

seLecteD BiBLioGRaphy

Numerous sources contributed to this text, but these are among the books I feel were the most helpful and enlightening:

Ann, Martha and Imel, Dorothy Myers. *Goddesses in World Mythology*. New York, NY: Oxford University Press, 1995.

Arrien, Angeles, Ph.D. *The Four-Fold Way*. New York, NY: Harper Collins Publishing, 1993.

Beyerl, Paul. *Herbal Magick*. Custer, WA: Phoenix Publishing, 1998.

Blackwolf, and Jones, Gina. *Earth Dance Drum*. Salt Lake City, UT: Commune-a-Key Publishing, 1996.

Bruce-Mitford, Miranda. *The Illustrated Book of Signs and Symbols*. London, England: DK Publishing, 1996.

Budapest, Z. *Grandmother of Time*. San Francisco, CA: Harper and Row, 1989.

Budge, E.A. Wallis. *Amulets and Superstitions*. Oxford, England: Oxford University Press, 1930.

Cowan, Tom. *Shamanism*. Freedom, CA: The Crossing Press, 1996.

Cruden, Loren. *Compass of the Heart*. Rochester, VT: Destiny Books, 1996.

Drury, Nevill. *The Elements of Shamanism*. Ringwood, Victoria, Australia: Element Books, 1997.

Gordon, Stuart. *Encyclopedia of Myths and Legends*. London, England: Headline Books, 1993.

Harner, Michael. *The Way of the Shaman.* New York, NY: Harper Collins Publishers, 1990.

Henderson, Helene, and Thompson, Sue Ellen, eds. *Holidays, Festivals, and Celebrations of the World Dictionary.* Detroit, MI: Omnigraphics, Inc. 1997.

Jordan, Michael. *Encyclopedia of Gods.* New York, NY: Facts on File, Inc. 1993.

Kalweit, Holger. *Dreamtime and Inner Space.* Boston, MA: Shambhala Publications, 1988.

King, Serge Kahili. *Urban Shaman.* New York, NY: Fireside Books, 1990.

Leach, Maria, ed. *Standard Dictionary of Folklore, Mythology and Legend.* New York, NY: Funk and Wagnall, 1984.

Leach, Marjorie. *Guide to the Gods.* Santa Barbara, CA: ABC-Clio, 1992.

Lurker, Manfred. *Dictionary of Gods and Goddesses, Devils and Demons.* New York, NY: Routledge and Kegan Paul Ltd., 1995.

Meadows, Kenneth. *The Medicine Way.* Rockport, MA: Element Books, 1990.

Mitford, Miranda Bruce. *Illustrated Book of Signs and Symbols.* New York, NY: DK Publishing, 1996.

Rutherford, Leo. *Principles of Shamanism.* San Francisco, CA: Harper Collins Publishers, 1996.

"Round and round the world, life is a masquerade." *The Smithsonian,* December 1994 issue, Washington DC, 1994.

Sams, Jamie, and Carson, David. *Medicine Cards*. Santa Fe, NM: Bear and Company, 1988.

Steiger, Brad. *Totems*. San Francisco CA: Harper Collins, 1996.

Summer Rain, Mary. *Earthway*. New York, NY: Pocket Books. 1990.

Telesco, Patricia. *Herbal Arts*. Secaucus, NJ: Carol Publishing, 1998.

Telesco, Patricia. *Kitchen Witch's Cookbook*. St. Paul, MN: Llewellyn Publications, 1994.

Telesco, Patricia. *Urban Pagan*. St. Paul, MN: Llewellyn Publications, 1993.

Van Lann, Nancy. *In a Circle, Long Ago*. New York, NY: Alfred A. Knopf, 1995.

Walker, Barbara. *The Woman's Dictionary of Symbols and Sacred Objects*. San Francisco, CA: Harper & Row, 1988.

Waring, Philippa. *The Dictionary of Omens and Superstitions*. Secaucus, NJ: Chartwell Books, 1978.

Wolfe, Amber. *The Truth About Shamanism*. St. Paul, MN: Llewellyn Publications, 1991.

Woodhead, Henry (series editor). *The Spirit World*. Alexandria, VA: Time Life Books, 1992.

BOOKS BY THE CROSSING PRESS

OTHER BOOKS BY PATRICIA TELESCO

A Little Book of Love Magic

A cornucopia of lore, magic, and imaginative ritual designed to bring excitement and romance to your life. Patricia Telesco tells us how to use magic to manifest our hopes and dreams for romantic relationships, friendships, family relations, and passions for our work.

$9.95 • Paper • ISBN 0-89594-887-7

FutureTelling: A Complete Guide to Divination

This cross-cultural encyclopedia of divination practices gives over 250 entries, from simple signs and omens of traditional folk magic to complex rituals of oracular consultation.

$16.95 • Paper • ISBN 0-89594-872-9

Ghosts, Spirits and Hauntings

Ghosts, specters, phantoms, shades, spooks, or wraiths-no matter what the name, Patricia Telesco will help you identify and cope with their presence. Whatever you encounter, Patricia would like you to relate to it sensitively and intelligently, using this book as a guide.

$10.95 • Paper • ISBN 0-89594-871-0

The Language of Dreams

Patricia Telesco outlines a creative, interactive approach to understanding the dream symbols of our inner life. Interpretations of more than 800 dream symbols incorporate multi-cultural elements with psychological, religious, folk, and historical meanings.

$16.95 • Paper • ISBN 0-89594-836-2

Spinning Spells, Weaving Wonders: Modern Magic for Everyday Life

This essential book of over 300 spells tells how to work with simple, easy-to-find components and focus creative energy to meet daily challenges with awareness, confidence, and humor.

$14.95 • Paper • ISBN 0-89594-803-6

Wishing Well: Empowering Your Hopes and Dreams

Blending folklore, magic, and creative visualization, author Patricia Telesco explains how reclaiming the practice of Wishcraft can create our reality exactly as we wish it to be.

$14.95 • Paper • ISBN 0-89594-870-2

BOOKS BY THE CROSSING PRESS

OTHER BOOKS BY THE CROSSING PRESS

A Woman's I Ching

By Diane Stein

A feminist interpretation of the popular ancient text for diving the character of events. Stein's version reclaims the feminine, or yin, content of the ancient work and removes all oppressive language and imagery.

$16.95 • Paper • ISBN 0-89594-857-5

All Women Are Psychics

By Diane Stein

Women's intuition is no myth; women really are psychic. But your inborn psychic sense was probably suppressed when you were very young. This inspiring book will help you rediscover and reclaim your dormant psychic aptitude.

$16.95 • Paper • ISBN 0-89594-979-2

Channeling for Everyone: A Safe Step-by-Step Guide to Developing Your Intuition and Psychic Awareness

By Tony Neate

This is a clear, concise guide to developing our subtler levels of consciousness. It provides us with safe, step-by-step exercises to prepare for and begin to practice channeling, allowing wider states of consciousness to become part of our everyday lives.

$12.95 • Paper • ISBN 0-89594-922-9

Clear Mind, Open Heart: Healing Yourself, Your Relationships and the Planet

By Eddie and Debbie Shapiro

The Shapiros offer an uplifting, inspiring, and deeply sensitive approach to healing through spiritual awareness. Includes practical exercises and techniques to help us all in making our own journey.

$16.95 • Paper • ISBN 0-89594-917-2

Fundamentals of Hawaiian Mysticism

By Charlotte Berney

Evolving in isolation on an island paradise, the mystical practice of Huna has shaped the profound yet elegantly simple Hawaiian character. Charlotte Berney presents Huna traditions as they apply to words, prayer, gods, the breath, a loving spirit, family ties, nature, and mana.

$12.95 • Paper • ISBN 1-58091-026-2

BOOKS BY THE CROSSING PRESS

Fundamentals of Jewish Mysticism and Kabbalah
By Ron Feldman

This concise introductory book explains what Kabbalah is and how study of its text and practices enhance the life of the soul and the holiness of the body.

$12.95 • Paper • ISBN 1-58091-049-1

Fundamentals of Tibetan Buddhism
By Rebecca McClen Novick

This book explores the history, philosophy, and practice of Tibetan Buddhism. Novick's concise history of Buddhism, and her explanations of the Four Noble Truths, Wheel of Life, Karma, Five Paths, Six Perfections, and the different schools of thought within the Buddhist teachings help us understand Tibetan Buddhism as a way of experiencing the world, more than as a religion or philosophy.

$12.95 • Paper • ISBN 0-89594-953-9

The Heart of the Circle: A Guide to Drumming
By Holly Blue Hawkins

Holly Blue Hawkins will walk you through the process of finding a drum, taking care of it, calling a circle, setting an intention, and drumming together. She will also show you how to incorporate drumming into your spiritual practice. She offers you an invitation to explore rhythm in a free and spontaneous manner.

$12.95 • Paper • ISBN 1-58091-025-4

The Native American Sweat Lodge: History and Legends
By Joseph Bruchac

To deepen our understanding of the significance of sweat lodges within Native American cultures, Bruchac shares 25 relevant traditional tales from the Lakota, Blackfoot, Hopi, and others.—Booklist

$12.95 • Paper • ISBN 0-89594-636-X

Peace Within the Stillness:
Relaxation & Meditation for True Happiness
By Eddie and Debbie Shapiro

Meditation teachers Eddie and Debbie Shapiro teach a simple, ancient practice which will enable you to release even deeper levels of inner stress and tension. Once you truly relax, you will enter the quiet mind and experience the profound, joyful, and healing energy of meditation.

$14.95 • Paper • ISBN 0-89594-926-1

BOOKS BY THE CROSSING PRESS

Physician of the Soul: *A Modern Kabbalist's Approach to Health and Healing*

By Rabbi Joseph H. Gelberman with Lesley Sussman

In a self-awareness program suitable for all faiths, internationally renowned Rabbi Joseph Gelberman reveals wisdom drawn from Jewish mysticism. Exercises in meditation, visualization, and prayer are discussed to promote harmony in mind, body, and soul.

$14.95 • Paper • ISBN 1-58091-061-0

Pocket Guide to Celtic Spirituality

By Sirona Knight

The Earth-centered philosophy and rituals of ancient Celtic spirituality have special relevance today as we strive to balance our relationship with the planet. This guide offers a comprehensive introduction to the rich religious tradition of the Celts.

$6.95 • Paper • ISBN 0-89594-907-5

Pocket Guide to Meditation

By Alan Pritz

This book focuses on meditation as part of spiritual practice, as a universal tool to forge a deeper connection with spirit. In Alan Pritz's words, Meditation simply delivers one of the most purely profound experiences of life, joy.

$6.95 • Paper • ISBN 0-89594-886-9

Pocket Guide to Self Hypnosis

By Adam Burke, Ph. D.

Self-hypnosis and imagery are powerful tools that activate a very creative quality of mind. By following the methods provided, you can begin to make progress on your goals and feel more in control of your life and destiny.

$6.95 • Paper • ISBN 0-89594-824-9

Shamanism as a Spiritual Practice for Daily Life

By Tom Cowan

This inspirational book blends elements of shamanism with inherited traditions and contemporary religious commitments. An inspiring spiritual call.—Booklist

$16.95 • Paper • ISBN 0-89594-838-9

To receive a current catalog from The Crossing Press
please call toll-free, 800-777-1048.
Visit our Web site: **www.crossingpress.com**